Better Homes and Gardens®

CROCHETING & KNITTING

BETTER HOMES AND GARDENS® BOOKS

Editorial Director: Don Dooley
Executive Editor: Gerald Knox
Art Director: Ernest Shelton
Assistant Art Director: Randall Yontz
Production and Copy Editor: David Kirchner
Craft Editor: Nancy Lindemeyer
Senior Associate Craft Editor: Ciba Vaughan
Associate Craft Editor: Marie B. Schulz
Graphic Designers: Sheryl Veenschoten,
Faith Berven, Harijs Priekulis

CONTENTS

Our collection of afghans was selected to suit a variety of tastes and moods. There are both old-fashioned and contemporary designs in colors that range from bold and brilliant hues to light and tantalizing pastel tints.

Complement your tableware with handmade table covers, and you'll dine in style. This selection runs the gamut from reproductions of exquisite old lace to quick and easy place mats of jute and string.

Whether you're decorating a master bedroom, a child's room, or a nursery, handmade crocheted or knitted bedspreads and pillows will add a stamp of individuality to make you happy whenever you enter the room.

Handcrafted Rugs _____ 54-67

Here's your chance to learn how to make area, accent, and scatter rugs that fit your rooms and flatter your furnishings. Use yarn, recycled materials, or even jute to create crocheted and knitted rugs in the colors you wish.

Accessories _____ 68-85

Add that extra special touch to your decor with baskets, pillows, doilies, or even casement curtains that you crochet or knit yourself. These small items also make ideal gifts for loved ones.

Glossary _____ 86-95

In addition to the basic crochet and knitting stitches, the glossary includes instructions for the granny square sampler afghan shown on pages 4-5. Once you master these techniques, you'll be ready to tackle intriguing projects for your home.

Designers and Acknowledgments _____ 96

Crocheting and knitting are both needle arts that enable you to create warm, wonderful things for your home. In this book you will find many such projects, just waiting for you to make.

Afghans

Top on the list of popular projects for knitters and crocheters alike are afghans. And no wonder, when you realize how a brightly colored afghan can cozy and personalize a room just by being there. The afghan spread out before you here is in the popular granny tradition, and this particular one is a sampler of the many different types of granny squares. You may crochet an afghan exactly like this one (see page 86 for complete instructions), or you can make a complete afghan from any one of the squares—as you'll see illustrated on the following pages with the star motif afghan.

Crocheted Star Motif Afghan

With just one motif—this patriotic star from the afghan shown on the preceding pages—you can make a spectacular afghan like the one pictured at right. Size is 40x54 inches, less fringe.

Materials

4 ply acrylic knitting worsted, 4 oz. skeins
1 yellow
2 blue
2 red
5 white
Size H aluminum crochet hook

Directions

Note: Afghan is made of 35 squares: 18 blue stars with alternating red and blue borders, and 17 red stars with alternating blue and red borders. Each star motif is 8 inches square. Stars have yellow centers (Rnd. 1), Rnds. 4, 7, and 9 are all white.

Basic star square—Starting with yellow, ch 3, sl st to 1st ch to form ring, ch 1. Rnd 1: * 1 sc in center of ring, ch 4, 1 sc in 2nd chain from hook, 1 sc in each of next 2 ch sts, rep from * 4 more times (5 spoke star center); join with sl st to beg sc. End off.

Rnd 2: Attach mc in center top st of any spoke, ch 1, sc in same sp, * sk next 3 sc, (1 trc, 1 dc, 1 trc) in next sc, sl st to top of next spoke, rep from * around; join with sl st to beg sc. *Do not end off.*

Rnd 3: * sk next st, (1 hdc, 1 dc, 1 trc, ch 1, 1 trc, 1 dc, 1 hdc) in top of next st, sk next st, sl st in top of next st, rep from * around; join with sl st to beg st. End off.

Rnd 4: Attach white in ch 1 back loop st of any point, * sk next 3 sts, (1 trc, 3 dc, 1 trc) in next st, sk next 3 sts, sl st in back loop of ch 1 point, rep from

* around; join with sl st to beg st. End off.

Rnd 5: Attach 2nd color in any st, (work through both loops), 2 sc in each st around (60 sc); join with sl st to beg sc. End off.

Rnd 6: (*Note:* Work on right side in top back loops only.) With star point at top, count clockwise 8 sc sts from point (this will be in sc above 3rd dc in rnd 4). Attach mc, work ch 6, 1 trc in next sc, * 1 dc in next sc, 1 hdc in each of next 2 sc, 1 sc in each of next 7 sc, 1 hdc in each of next 2 sc, 1 dc in next sc, 1 trc in next sc, ch 2, 1 trc in next sc, rep from * around; join with sl st to top of 4th ch of beg ch 6. End off.

Rnd 7: Attach white in ch 2 corner sp, ch 3, 1 sc in same sp, * 1 sc each in next 15 sts, 1 sc in next ch 2 sp, rep from * around; join with sl st to beg sc. End off.

Rnd 8: Attach 2nd color in ch 2 corner, rep rnd 7 (17 sc on each side).

Rnd 9: Attach white in any corner sp, (ch 2, 1 hdc, ch 3, 2 hdc) in same sp, * sk next sc, 2 hdc in next sc, rep from * across to next corner, * work (2 hdc, ch 3, 2 hdc) in same corner sp, rep from * around; join with sl st to top of beg ch 2. End off.

Assembling—Alternate blue and red squares. Attach rows together on right side with white, working with sl st.

Border—(*Note:* Alternate rows of white, red, and white.)

Rows 1, 2, and 3: Work 2 hdc bet groups of hdc along all edges, and (2 hdc, ch 3, 2 hdc) in each corner.

Fringe—Use double strands of 9-inch-long white yarn. Fold in half, and with crochet hook, knot around edges of afghan between each hdc group.

Grandmother's Flower Garden Afghan

This familiar patchwork quilt pattern can also be made into a most attractive crocheted afghan. Worked up in springtime colors, the afghan brings a flower garden atmosphere to your home all year 'round. Use any colors you fancy to whip up this quick and easy crochet—a perfect pick-up-and-go project worked one "petal" motif at a time. Another plus for the Grandmother's Flower Garden pattern—it provides an ideal way to use leftover yarn pieces.

The finished measurements for our afghan are 48x60 inches.

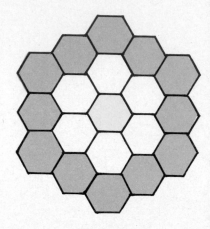

Materials
Knitting worsted, 4 oz. skeins
  9 green (G)
  1 yellow (Y)
  1 flame
  1 blue (variegated)
  1 coral
  1 gold
  1 rust (variegated)
  1 pale yellow
  1 med. blue
  1 pink
  1 lt. blue
  1 multicolor (variegated)
Size F crochet hook

Gauge
Each motif measures 3½ inches point to point.

Directions
Note: Crochet 145 green motifs for the background, 18 motifs in yellow for flower centers, and 6 motifs (all one color) for each of the 18 flowers.

Pattern stitch—To make cluster, yo hook and draw up loop, yo and draw up another loop, (five strands on hook), yo and draw through all loops on hook, ch 1. One cluster made.

Hexagonal motif—Ch 6, join with sl st to form ring, ch 1. Rnd. 1: Work 6 cluster sts in ring; join in top of first cluster with sl st, ch 1.

Rnd. 2: In first sp between clusters of previous row, make 2 cluster sts. Proceeding around, make 2 clusters in each sp. (There should be 6 *double* clusters.) Join with sl st, ch 1.

Rnd. 3: Make one cluster in space between double clusters of previous row. Proceeding around, make double clusters over previous doubles, and a single cluster in the space between. (There should be 6 double alternating with 6 single clusters.)

Rnd. 4: Keeping double clusters over previous double clusters, and single clusters in the spaces between, continue around. Join with sl st, break off yarn and weave in loose end.

Finishing—Whipstitch all the motifs together with the green background color, following the diagram for placement. Finish the edge with 2 rows of sc in green all around.

Classic Americana Pattern

This lovely old design is equally as beautiful in today's homes as it was in the stately residences of days gone by. Crochet it as an afghan for your sofa, or as a coverlet for a twin-size or double bed. Directions are given first for a 48x62-inch afghan, with 66x102-inch twin bed and 76x102-inch double bed sizes in parentheses. (These sizes do not include the fringe, which adds several inches.)

Materials

Bernat Berella, "4," 4 oz. balls
  18 (21-27) off-white
Size G crochet hook

Gauge

4 dc = 1 inch
Note: Entire afghan is worked in back loop only.

Directions

Pattern stitch for shell—Row 1: 1 dc in 4th ch from hook, 1 dc in same st, skip next 2 sts, 1 sc in next st, skip next 2 sts, * 5 dc in next st (shell), skip next 2 sts, 1 sc in next st, skip next 2 sts, repeat from * across row, ending 3 dc in last st (half shell)—29 (40-45) shells and 2 half shells.

Row 2: Ch 1, turn, working in back loop only, 1 shell in next sc, * 1 sc in 3rd dc of next shell, 1 shell in next sc, repeat from *, ending 1 sc in top of turning ch —30 (41-46) shells. Row 3: Ch 3, turn, 2 dc in first st, * 1 sc in 3rd dc of next shell, 1 shell in next sc, repeat from *, ending 3 dc in top of turning ch — 29 (40-45) shells and 2 half shells. (Always count ch 3 as first dc.) Repeat rows 2 and 3 for pattern stitch.

Pattern stitch for dc—Row 1: Ch 3, turn, working in back loop only, 1 dc in each st across row — 181 (247-277) sts. Repeat row 1 for pattern stitch.

Pattern stitch for bobble— Row 1: Ch 3, turn, working in back loop only, 1 dc in each of next 4 dc, * 5 dc in next st, remove hook from st, insert hook in back loop of first st of 5 dc just made and draw loop of last st through loop on hook (back loop bobble), 1 dc in each of next 5 dc, repeat from *, ending back loop bobble in next st, 1 dc in turning ch — 30 (41-46) bobbles.

Row 2: Ch 3, turn, 1 dc in each of next 3 sts, * 5 dc in next st, remove hook from st, insert hook in front loop of first st of 5 dc just made and draw loop of last st through loop on hook (front loop bobble), 1 dc in each of next 5 sts, repeat from *, ending front loop bobble in next st, 1 dc in next st, 1 dc in turning ch. Bobbles will be on right side.

Repeat rows 1 and 2 for pattern st. Ch 184 (250-280) sts. Work in pattern st as follows: 8 rows shell pattern. 8 rows dc pattern. 8 rows bobble pattern. 8 rows dc pattern.

Repeat these 32 rows 3 times more for small size afghan only. Do not fasten off. For medium and large size coverlets only, repeat these 32 rows 4 times more, ending 8 rows shell pattern, 9 rows dc pattern. Do not fasten off.

Edging—For all sizes: With right side facing you, * 5 dc in turning ch of next row (shell), 1 sc in last st of next row, skip 1 row, repeat from * to first corner, working 1 shell in corner st. Work same edging on remaining lower and side edges. Fasten off. Fringe—Cut strands of yarn 10 inches long, knot 10 strands in space between 2nd and 3rd st of shell st on 3 sides of afghan. Trim ends. Steam lightly.

Brilliant Flower Patch Afghan

Using the afghan stitch—an easy crocheting technique—you can create this stunning afghan a square at a time. After each square is completed, you simply embroider on a whopping big flower in bright sunshine shades (see chart on page 14 for floral motifs). Finished size is about 44x76 inches.

Materials

Bernat Sesame, "4," 4 oz. balls
  12 white main color (MC)
   3 lt. olive (color A)
   3 dk. olive (color B)
   1 goldenrod (color C)
   1 orange (color D)
  or
Bernat Berella Germantown, 4 oz. balls
  12 white main color (MC)
   3 lt. olive (color A)
   3 dk. olive (color B)
   1 honey color (color C)
   1 orange (color D)
Size H afghan hook
Size E crochet hook

Gauge

9 sts = 2 inches, 4 rows = 1 inch

Directions

Afghan stitch—Row 1: Draw up a loop in each st of ch, leaving all loops on hook (Fig. 1); take off loops as follows. Yo hook, draw through 1 loop, * yo draw through 2 loops, repeat from * across row (Fig. 2); the loop remaining on hook counts as first loop of next row (Fig. 3).

Row 2: Skip first upright bar (Fig. 3). Draw up a loop in next and each remaining upright bar (Fig. 4), leaving all loops on hook; take off loops in same manner as row 1. Repeat row 2 only for specified length.

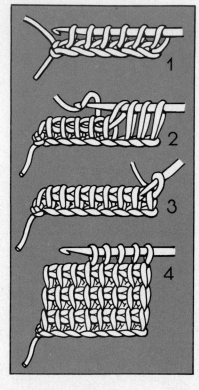

Squares—Make 15. Using MC and afghan hook, ch 63 sts. Work even in afghan st for 51 rows. Work 1 sl st in each upright bar. Fasten off.

Border—Using crochet hook, join color A at top right-hand corner, ch 1, 2 sc in same st, * 1 sc in each of next 61 sts, 3 sc in corner st, 1 sc in each row (50 sc), 3 sc in corner st, repeat from * around, join with sl st to top of ch 1.

Rnd. 2: Ch 1, turn, * 1 sc in each st to corner, 3 sc in corner st, ** 1 sc in each of next 5 sts, sk 1 st, rep from ** to next corner st, 3 sc in corner st, rep from * around, join—54 sts on each side. Rnds. 3 and 4: Ch 1, turn, 1 sc in each st and 3 sc in each corner st. Rnd. 5: Fasten off color A, pull color B through loop on hook and work 1 sc in each st and 3 sc in each corner st. Fasten off.

Cross stitch design—Following chart, work cross stitch designs on afghan stitch squares in the following manner.

Each upright bar across row of afghan st is counted as 1 st. Following the chart, count the upright bars. You will note that there are two holes formed by afghan st after each upright bar.

Working from left to right, join color on wrong side at lower hole and work across next upright bar to upper hole. Then bring needle through lower hole directly below (Fig 5). Continue on number of sts for color being used. Then work from right to left to form cross (Fig. 6). Be careful not to pull too tightly.

Make 8 squares with color C flowers and 7 in color D, alternating colors.

Finishing—Make 5 strips. Using color B, overcast 3 squares tog. Then overcast the 5 strips tog. Using color B, work in sc, working 3 sc in each corner st. Fasten off.

Fringe—Cut strands of color B 15 inches long. Knot 1 strand in each st across each short end of afghan. Trim ends. Steam lightly.

continued

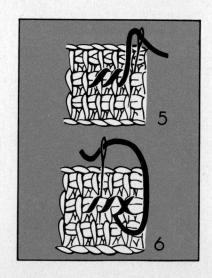

Brilliant Flower Patch Afghan *(continued)*

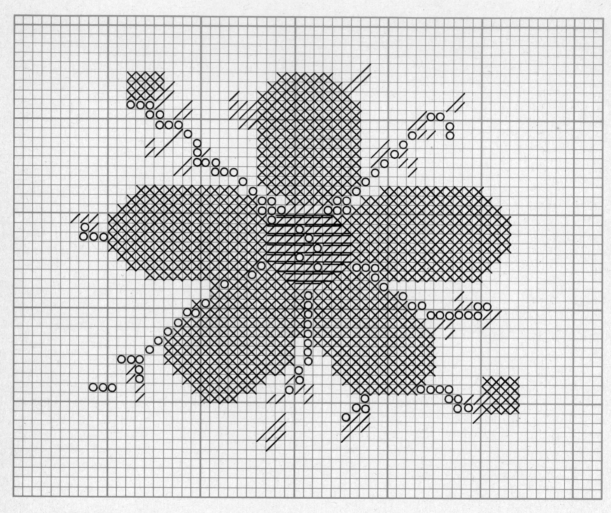

KEY TO CHART

□ = White Main Color (MC)

/ = Lt. Olive (Color A)

O = Dk. Olive (Color B)

X = Goldenrod (Color C)

Z = Orange (Color D)

Cozy Quilt-Patterned Throw

Here's a fabulous way to use leftover yarn. For this easy-to-knit afghan, collect sport-weight yarn in a variety of colors. As you knit each triangle (using garter stitch), combine your yarn with ecru knitting worsted. The results of your efforts produce this lovely variegated crayon effect.

Materials

Knitting worsted, 4 oz. skeins
  10 ecru
  10 colors sport-weight yarn
Size 10½ knitting needles

Gauge

Each square measures 6½ inches

Directions

The entire afghan is worked in garter st, k every row.

Working with two strands of yarn, ecru plus one of the colors of yarn, cast on 2 sts.

Row 1: Inc 1 st, k across row. Rep 13 times; break off color and add a second color. Rep row 1 four more times. Bind off rem 20 sts.

Work 256 triangles in same manner. Whipstitch four triangles tog to form squares. Join eight squares in each strip. Join the eight strips together. See picture insert for finished design.

Quick Knit Patchwork Afghan

This afghan, with its simple garter stitch squares in bold and vibrant colors, is completely contemporary. So if you're looking for a work-up-fast project, in tune with today's casual life-style, you'll want to try this one. It's virtually a no-fail design, even for beginners. Smashing striped squares add just enough challenge and interest to keep any knitter going great guns. This afghan measures approximately 47x47 inches.

Materials

Unger's Nanette, 1¾ oz. ball
  3 red (A)
  3 green (B)
  3 orange (C)
  3 blue (D)
  6 off-white (E)
Size 10 knitting needles

Gauge

4 sts = 1 inch. Each block to measure 5 inches square

Directions

Pattern St—Garter st (k every row).

Solid squares—With size 10 needles, cast on 20 sts. Work even in garter st for 5 inches. Bind off. Make 11 squares in each of the 5 colors A, B, C, D and E—55 squares.

Striped squares—With size 10 needles and any contrasting color (A, B, C or D), cast on 20 sts. K 5 rows. Fasten off. * Attach E and k 6 rows with E; attach contrast color and k 6 rows with the contrasting color; rep from * until there are 8 stripes in all.

Break yarn after each color change. Attach contrast color and k 5 rows. Bind off. Make 11 striped squares in each of colors A, B, C and D combined with E— 44 squares.

Short bands—Make 2. With size 10 needles and E, cast on 180 sts. Work garter st for ¾ inch. Bind off.

Long bands—Make 2. With size 10 needles and E, cast on 228 sts. Work garter st for ¾ inch. Bind off.

Finishing—Arrange squares as shown or as desired. Alternate striped squares, using some with stripe in a horizontal position and others with stripe in a vertical position. Alternate solid squares with garter st in a horizontal position and others in a vertical position. Arrange colors to suit your individual taste. Sew squares tog on wrong side, taking in a small amount on the seam. Sew 9 squares across for width and 11 squares for length. Sew bands in place, matching corners. Steam lightly on wrong side. Do not press.

KNITTING TIPS

■ *When you are joining a new ball of yarn, always join at the outer edge. With the new strand, make a slip knot around the strand you are knitting with. Then move the slip knot up to the edge of your work and continue knitting with the newly attached strand. (Knot will thus be concealed in a seam instead of in the body of your garment where it might show.)*

■ *When you are working with more than one color, always pick up the color you are about to use from underneath the dropped strand. This prevents holes as you are changing colors.*

South-of-the-Border Style Afghan

Imagine what a fiesta-like, handmade afghan can do for your sofa! To add just the right dramatic flare, knit this handsome afghan of easy-to-make garter stitch squares. Then to finish, join the squares in the intriguing diagonal fashion shown opposite. The finished size is approximately 40x70 inches, not including the thick, deep fringe.

Materials
Bucilla "Wool and Shetland Wool," 2 oz. balls or Bear Brand, Fleisher's or Botany Machine Washable Winsom, 2 oz. skeins

    15 black (A)
    4 white (B)
    2 orange (C)
    1 green (D)
    1 scarlet (E)
    1 turquoise (F)
    1 purple (G)
Size 10 knitting needles
Yarn markers

Gauge
Each finished square should measure about 4½x4½ inches. Afghan consists of 112 squares —52 (A), 26 (B), 10 (C) and 6 each (D, E, F and G).

Directions
Square—Cast on 35 sts loosely. Row 1: wrong side—With yarn at back, sl first st as to p, k 33, p last st. *Note:* SKP means s1, k1, and pass sl st over. Row 2: Sl 1, k 14, SKP, place marker on right needle, k l, k next 2 sts tog, k 14, p 1; 33 sts. Carry marker.

Note: On every row, with yarn at back, sl first st as if to p and p last st.

Row 3: Sl 1, k 31, p 1. Row 4: Sl 1, k to within 2 sts of marker, SKP, sl marker, k 1, k next 2 sts tog, k to within 1 st of end, p 1; 31 sts. Row 5: Sl 1, k to within 1 st of end, p 1. Repeat rows 4 and 5, 13 times, end on wrong side; 5 sts. Row 32: SKP, drop marker, k 1, k 2 tog; 3 sts. Row 33: Sl 1, k 1, p 1. Row 34: Sl 1, k 2 tog, pass sl st over the k 2 tog, fasten off. Mark for lower point.

Finishing—Block each square to about 4½x4½ inches. Arrange squares as shown on chart at bottom of page, with care to have all squares in same position. From right side, with care to keep seams elastic, sew squares tog with weaving st. Steam lightly.

Fringe—Wind A around 7-, 8-, and 9-inch-wide pieces of cardboard (three different lengths of strands are used for fringe). Cut at one end as shown in drawing No. 1 at right.

Note: Knot 4 strands of given length for each fringe. (See drawing No. 2.)

With the shortest strands, knot one fringe at each of the outer points. With the longest length strands, knot one fringe at each of the inner points. Knot 9 fringes evenly spaced between as follows: 3 with the shortest length strands at either side of the outer point; 3 with the longest length strands at either side of the inner point; and 3 with medium length strands in between.

At the four corners, with the shortest length strands, knot one fringe at each point and at each seam—9 fringes evenly spaced in between. Trim evenly.

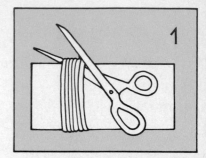

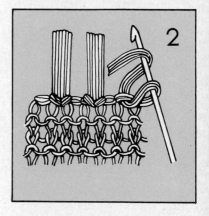

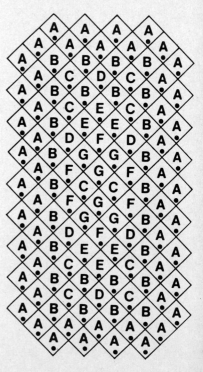

Old-Fashioned "Windowpane" Knitted Afghan

This puff stitch afghan has much of the beauty of stained window glass, because of the fascinating way bits of brilliant yarn colors are used. In fact, colors that would not ordinarily look well next to each other become harmonious because of the black yarn similar to the leading in stained glass that separates the colorful "panes" and forms the puffs at the same time.

This afghan measures about 46x70 inches.

Materials

Knitting Worsted, 4 oz. skeins
  2 black
  An assortment of colors that totals approximately 18 ounces
Size 10½ 29-inch circular knitting needle
Size F crochet hook

Gauge

4 sts = 1 inch, 6 rows = 1 inch

Directions

With black yarn, cast on 128 sts. Work 4 rows in st st (k 1 row, p 1 row). Tie in the first color and work 6 rows in st st.

Tie in black, k 4, * ravel or drop the next color st 6 rows down to the black. Put the right needle through the black loop from the front of work, then insert tip of right needle under horizontal rows of dropped sts, yo, pull under the horizontal rows and back through black loop to front of work again; place st last made on left needle and k 1 st. K 5 more sts, and rep from * Follow pattern across row, then p back with black.

Tie on another color and follow the instructions above.

Continue in this manner until the afghan is 60 inches long. End with 4 rows of black st st.

Crocheted edging—Work 1 row of sc around entire afghan, working 3 sc at each corner. (Total number should be a multiple of 10 plus 2.)

Pattern row—Sl st in first sc. * 1 sc in next sc, 1 hdc in next sc, 1 dc in next sc, 1 tr in next sc, 5 dtr in next sc, 1 tr in next sc, 1 dc in next sc, 1 hdc in next sc, 1 sc in next sc, sl st in next sc; rep from * to end. Fasten off.

KNITTING KNOW-HOW

■ Always buy enough yarn to complete your project, making sure the dye lot of each skein is the same. (Dye lots can vary.)

■ Always bind off stitches in the pattern of your garment or project, and work loosely to ensure "give" in the bound-off edge.

■ To pick up stitches, always work from the right side of your project. Using one needle only and a strand of yarn, insert the point of the needle through the knitting a short distance from the edge. Next wrap the yarn around the needle as if to knit, and draw the loop through the piece. Continue in this manner, spacing your stitches evenly.

■ If you drop a stitch, use a crochet hook to pick it up. In stockinette stitch, insert the hook through the loop of the dropped stitch from the front of the work to the back, with the hook facing upward. Pull the horizontal thread of the row above through the loop; repeat to the top and place dropped stitch on needle. If you are using a pattern stitch, pick up the stitch in the pattern.

Honeycomb Throw and Basket Stitch Pillow

Combine a solid color with a contrasting variegated yarn, add a little fancy stitchery, and you've got this unique throw and companion pillow. The throw measures about 48x58 inches, without fringe; the pillow is 14 inches.

Knit Throw

Materials

American Thread Co., Sayelle, 3½ oz. skeins
  5 burnt orange (A)
  6 blue variegated (B)
2 markers
Size 9 circular knitting needle
Size 4 crochet hook

Gauge

4½ sts = 1 inch, 6 rows = 1 inch

Directions

Note: Hexagon pattern has a multiple of 8 sts plus 6 (edge sts not counted in multiple).

Cast on 214 sts of color B. K 20 rows of garter st. (Separate 4 sts at each end by markers since they are always garter st and not included in directions.)

Row 1 hexagon pattern: Change to color A and k 6, * sl 2 as if to p, k 6 *, rep from * to * across row, end k 6.

Row 2: P 6, * hold yarn in front, sl 2 as if to p, p 6 *, rep from * to * across row, end p 6.

Rows 3 and 5: Same as row 1. Rows 4 and 6 same as row 2.

Rows 7, 8, 9, 10: Change to color B and k all sts, including sl sts in previous rows.

Row 11: Change to color A and k 2, * sl 2 as if to p, k 6 *, rep from * to *, end sl 2 as if to p, k 2.

Row 12: P 2, * sl 2 as if to p, p 6 *, rep from * to *, end sl 2 as if to p, k 2.

Rows 13 and 15: Same as row 11. Rows 14 and 16 same as row 12. Rows 17, 18, 19, 20: Same as rows 7, 8, 9 10.

Rep from row 1 through 20 until you have 19 pat repeats; rep rows 7 through 16. Change to color B and k 19 rows of garter st and cast off.

Finishing—At each end work one row of sc (cast on and cast off rows). Dampen throw in water to which fabric softener has been added (to avoid static electricity). Roll in towels to remove moisture, block to size.

Fringe—Cut 12-inch lengths of both color A and B for fringe. Use three strands for each unit. Leave about 1½ inches of space between each group of three strands. Trim fringe to an even length.

Note: Carry color of yarn not in use up right side by looping yarn in use around it so there isn't a long float of unused yarn.

Knitted Pillow

Materials

American Thread Co., Sayelle, 3½ oz. skeins
  1 burnt orange (A)
  1 blue variegated (B)
Size 9 knitting needles
14-inch-square pillow form

Gauge

5½ sts = 1 inch

Directions

Plaited basket st pat—uneven number of sts.

Row 1: K 2 * sk one st, k 2nd st, k 1st st, remove both sts from left needle *, rep from * to *, end k 1.

Row 2: P 2, * sk 1st st, p 2nd st, p 1st st, remove both sts from left needle *, rep from * to *, end p 1.

Cast on 77 sts of color B, p 1 row. * Work 4 rows of plaited basket st pat (rows 1, 2, 1, 2). Change to color A, work 4 rows in same pat (rows 1, 2, 1, 2) *. Rep from * to * 8 times, work 4 more rows in color B, cast off.

Work another piece, following the same instructions.

Finishing—Placing right sides tog, whipstitch around three sides, turn to right side, insert pillow, and whipstitch fourth side closed. *Note:* When sewing back and front tog, alternate ends so cast-on end is joined to cast-off end.

STITCH GAUGE

■ *When you see the word "gauge" at the beginning of a knit or crochet instruction, this is what it means. Gauge specifies how many stitches per inch you should have using a specified crochet hook or knitting needle. Since the sizing of any article is dependent upon this gauge, you must adjust your work to the given gauge or your finished article will not be the size indicated in the instructions.*

■ *Since everyone does not knit or crochet with the same tension, it is important to check your gauge before you start a project. Cast on or chain about 20 sts, using recommended yarn and needles or hook, and work about 4 inches in specified pattern. Bind or fasten off. Block swatch, then measure to see if rows and stitches correspond to required gauge.*

■ *If your stitch gauge is less than one given in instructions, try next size smaller needles or hook, and again check your gauge. If your stitch gauge is greater (more stitches per inch), try next size larger needle.*

For Your Table

Would you like to dress your table in an elegant downpour of lace, like the exquisite antique Victorian crocheted tablecloth pictured here? Or perhaps you'd rather go country with patterns that suggest heavy pottery, checks, and pretty prints? Well, whatever your style and your preference, you'll find beautiful, doable patterns to knit and crochet for your table in this section crammed with very special projects. For example, crocheters will delight in our jute place mats that are so easy even a beginner will be able to whip up one or more in just one sitting. And for experienced knitters, we present a challenge—knitted lace—an old art that is becoming very popular once again. The tablecloth shown on pages 28 and 29 features the lovely and popular apple blossom pattern. You may vary the size of any of our patterns to fit your own individual requirements. For complete instructions for the tablecloth at left, please turn the page.

Crochet Pattern from the Past *(shown on pages 24-25)*

Crocheted Lace Tablecloth

To re-create this fragile-looking Victorian lace tablecloth, you will need to crochet 210 round motifs and 182 joining motifs for a 5x5-foot tablecloth like the one shown in the photo on the preceding page.

Materials
Size 20 crochet thread
  13 balls ecru
Size 11 steel crochet hook

Directions
Ch 8, join with sl st to form a ring. Row 1: Ch 3 (counts as first dc), 23 dc in ring, sl st in top of first dc.

Row 2: * Ch 5, sk 1 dc, sl st once in each of next 2 dc *, rep from * 7 more times (there should be 8 loops on this round). End with a sl st in 1st st.

Row 3: Sl st to 3rd st of ch, ch 7, dc in same st * ch 4, dc in center st of next loop, ch 4, dc in same st (this makes a shell), rep from * 6 times, join with a sl st in top of first dc (there should be 16 sp on this rnd).

Row 4: Ch 1, 4 sc in next loop, sc in next dc, 4 sc in next loop, sc in next dc, rep around ending with a sl st in first sc.

Row 5: Ch 1, sc in next sc, sc in next sc, continue around ending with a sl st in first sc.

Rows 6, 7, and 8: Rep row 5.

Row 9: Ch 4, dc in next sc, ch 1, dc in next sc, ch 1, dc in next sc, rep around (there should be 78 dc on this round).

Row 10: Sl st in 1st sc, * ch 5, sk 2 sps, sl st in each of next 2 sps *, rep from * around. Join (there should be 20 loops on this rnd).

Row 11: Sl st to 3rd st of ch, ch 6, dc in same st, * ch 3, dc in center st of next loop, ch 3, dc in same st *. Rep from * around in pattern, ending with ch 3 and sl st in 3rd ch.

Row 12: Sl st into sp, ch 5, dc in same sp, ch 3, sc in next sp, ch 3, in next sp make dc, ch 3, dc (shell), ch 3, sc in next sp, ch 3; make shell in next sp. Rep in pattern, ending with a sl st in top of first dc.

Row 13: Rep row 12, making ch 4, sc in center sc, ch 4, bet shells. Break thread.

Joining—Join two motifs tog while working the last rnd. At any shell, make a dc on the second motif, ch 1, sl st in shell on first motif. Ch 1, dc in same sp as last dc on second motif, ch 3, dc in shell sp on second motif, ch 1, sl st in shell sp on first motif, ch 1, dc in shell on second motif, ch 3, dc in next shell. Ch 1, sl st in shell on first motif, ch 1, dc in shell on second motif.

Motifs for joining round medallions—Ch 5, join with sl st to form ring. Ch 15, sc bet 1st and 2nd motif, ch 15, sc in ring. Ch 10, sc in point on 2nd motif, ch 10, sc in ring. Ch 10, sc in point on 2nd motif, ch 10, sc in ring. Ch 15, sc bet 2nd and 3rd motif, ch 15, sc in ring.

Ch 10, sc in 3rd motif, ch 10, sc in ring. Ch 10, sc in 3rd motif, ch 10, sc in ring. Ch 15, sc bet 3rd and 4th motif, ch 15, sc in ring. Ch 10, sc in 4th motif, ch 10, sc in ring. Ch 10, sc in 4th motif, ch 10, sc in ring. Ch 15, sc bet 4th and 1st motif, ch 15, sc in ring. Ch 10, sc on 1st motif, ch 10, sc in ring. Ch 10, sc on 1st motif, ch 10, sc in ring. Break off thread.

Begin a tablecloth with a pattern of large and small medallions—like the ones pictured opposite—and crochet until you cover your table with these fresh, white "snowflakes." Directions given below are for a 5½-foot square, but you can make any size you wish. In fact, this pattern has wonderful possibilities for bedspreads, table runners, pillow tops, and even elegant lace curtains. And despite its intricate appearance, you'll be able to turn out many motifs in a single evening.

Materials
Bedspread cotton thread, 4 cord, 650 yd. balls
  7 white
Size 5 steel crochet hook

Directions
For a 5½-foot square, you will need 121 large medallions and 100 small medallions.

Large medallion—Ch 5, sl st in first ch to form ring.

Rnd 1: (Ch 10, sc in ring) 6 times.

Rnd 2: Sl st in ea of first 5 chs of ch 10 to bring thread into position. *Ch 8, sc in center st of next loop. Rep from * around, ending sl st in last sl st before first ch 8 (makes 6 spaces).

Rnd 3: Sl st in next ch. (Ch 3, 2 dc, ch 2, 3 dc) in first sp. *Ch 3, (3 dc, ch 2, 3 dc) in next sp. Rep from * around, ending ch 3; sl st to top of first ch 3.

Rnd 4: Sl st in ea of next 2 dc

and in first ch of ch 2. *Ch 8, sc in next ch 3 sp, ch 8, sc in next ch 2 sp. Rep from * around, ending sl st in base of first ch 8 (12 spaces).

Rnd 5: Ch 1, *(sc, hdc, dc, 3 trc, dc, hdc, sc) in first ch 8 sp. Sc in sc between loops. Rep around from *, ending sl st in sl st of rnd 4.

Rnd 6: Sl st in ea of next 5 sts. Sc in same sp as last sl st. *Ch 8, sc in center trc of next group. Rep from * around, ending sl st in first sc of rnd.

Rnd 7: Ch 1, *(sc, hdc, 7 dc, hdc, sc) in first ch 8 sp. Sc in sc between loops. Rep from * around ending sl st in sl st of rnd 6.

Rnd 8: Ch 6, sk 2 sts, dc in next st. *Ch 3, sk 2 sts, dc in next st. Rep from * around, ending ch 3, sl st in 3rd ch of ch 6 (48 spaces).

Rnd 9: Ch 6, dc in next dc, ch 3, dc in next dc, ch 3, dc in next dc. Ch 3, sl st in top of dc just made. Ch 5, sl st in same st. Ch 3, sl st in same st. (Triple picot). *Ch 3, dc in next dc, ch 3, dc in next dc, ch 3, dc in next dc, triple picot in top of last dc. Rep from * around ending with sl st in 3rd ch of ch 6 and triple picot in same st. End off (16 triple picots).

Joining large medallions— Make one large medallion as described. Make 2nd large medallion except attach it to first large medallion as follows: When making triple picot, ch 3, sl st to top of dc. Ch 2, sc thru long part of a picot of first medallion, ch 2, sl st in same sp with first ch 3.

Ch 3, sl st in same sp. (The two medallions are connected by their triple picots.) Join the two medallions in the same way by their next picots. Continue around as described for the first medallion. Join the other large medallions in the same way according to the diagram. When 4 large medallions have been connected in a square, insert a small medallion in the center.

Small medallion—Ch 5, sl st to first ch to form ring.

Rnds 1 & 2: Same as rnds 1 & 2 of large medallion.

Rnd 3: Sl st in ea of first 2 chs of ch 8. Ch 8, sk 3 ch, dc in next ch. Ch 5, dc in second ch of next ch 8. Rep around with dcs in 2nd and 6th chs of ea ch 8, and ch 5 between dcs. End sl st to 3rd ch of ch 6 (12 spaces).

Rnd 4: Ch 3, 2 dc in first sp. Triple picot in top of 2nd dc, 3 dc in same sp. Ch 1, 3 dc in next sp. Connect with large medallion by sc thru large part of picot. 3 dc in same sp. Ch 1, 3 dc in next sp, sc thru large part of next picot of large medallion, 3 dc in same ch 5 sp. Ch 1, (3 dc, triple picot, 3 dc) in next sp. Continue around connecting small medallion with all 4 large medallions and making a triple picot between the large medallions. End sl st to top of ch-3. End off.

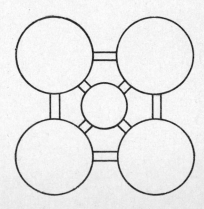

Knitted Lace Tablecloth

If you're an experienced knitter with a desire to do something different, try this challenging project. The pattern we feature here is the beautiful apple blossom design worked in ecru thread.

Materials

Knit-Cro-Sheen Thread, 550 yd. balls
  3 ecru
Size 2 double-pointed knitting needles (set of 5)
Size 4 16-inch circular knitting needle (for rows 25-59)
Size 6 29-inch circular knitting needle (for rows 60-191)
Size 4 crochet hook
Note: In order to simplify and abbreviate the basic knitting terms, the following abbreviations are used in this design:
O means yarn over
(O)2 means thread over twice
Skb means slip 1, knit 1, pass slip stitch over
N means narrow (knit 2 tog)
Snb means slip 1, knit 2 tog, pass slip stitch over
V 2 means to increase by knitting in front and in back of stitch
K1b means to knit in back of stitch
V 3 means to increase by knitting in front, in back, and in front of stitch

Directions

With crochet hook, ch 5. Join. Sc 8 sts in circle. Hook through both loops, draw up and place on knitting needles, 2 sts on each of 4 double-pointed needles. *Note:* K plain all rows that are not numbered. Insert a marker so you can tell where each rnd begins. Repeat the directions for each row around entire row.
  Row 1: K. Row 3: K. Row 5: K 1, o. Row 7: k 1, o, k 1, o.

Row 9: (k 1, o) 4 times.
Rows: 11, 12, 13, 14: P. Row 15: K. Row 16: (k 1, o) 8 times.
Row 18: K 16, o. Row 20: K 4, (o, skb) 4 times, k 3, n.
Row 22: K 16, o. Row 24: K 2 (o, skb) 6 times, k 1, n.
Row 26: K 16, o. Row 28: K 4 (o, skb) 4 times, k 3, n.
Row 30: K 16, o. Row 32: K 6 (o, skb) twice, k 5, n.
Row 34: K 3, o, k 10, o, k 3, o.
Row 36: K 19. Row 38: K 10, o, k 9, o.
Row 40: K 21. Row 42: K 5, o, k 11, o, k 5, o. Row 44: K 24.
Row 46: K 12, o, k 12, o.
Row 48: K 26 (o) twice. Row 50: K 26, o, k 2, o. Row 52: K 26, o, k 4, o. Row 54: K 26, o, k 1, n (o) twice, skb, k 1, o. Row 56: K 26, o, n, (o) twice, skb, n, (o) twice, skb, o.
Row 58: Skb, k 22, n, o, k 3, n (o) twice, skb, k 3, o.
Row 60: O, skb, [n (o) twice, skb] 8 times, n, o.
Row 62: O, n, o, (o, skb, n, o) three times, skb, n, o, (o, skb, n, o) four times, o, skb (There is only one yarn over after the first group of three).
Row 64: O, k 1, o, k 2, [n (o) twice, skb] three times, k 1, n, o, k 1, o, skb, k 1, [n (o) twice, n] three times, k 2.
Row 66: O, k 3, o, [n (o) twice, skb] four times.
Row 68: O, k 5, o, k 2, [n (o) twice, skb] three times, k 2.
Row 70: O, k 7, o, skb, k 2, [n (o) twice, skb] twice, k 2, n. Row 72: O, k 9, o, skb, k 3, n, (o) twice, skb, k 3, n.
Row 74: O, k 11, o, k 2 [n (o) twice, skb] twice, k 2.
Row 76: K 13, o, [n (o) twice, skb] three times, o.
Row 78: K 5, snb, k 5, o, k 3 [n (o) twice, skb] twice, k 3, o.
Row 80: K 4, snb, k 4, o, k 2, [n (o) twice, skb] three times, k 2, o. Row 82: K 3, snb, k 3, o, k 1, [n (o) twice, n], four times, k 1, o.
Row 84: K 2, snb, k 2, o, [n (o)

twice, skb] five times, o.
Row 86: K 1, snb, k 1, o, k 3, [n (o) twice, skb] four times, k 3, o. Row 88: Snb, o, k 2, [n (o) twice, skb] five times, k 2, o. Row 90: K1b, k 1, [n (o) twice, n] six times, k 1, o.
Row 92: [n (o) twice, n] seven times. Row 94: O, skb, [n (o) twice, skb] six times, n, o.
Row 96: [n (o) twice, n] seven times.
Row 98: O, skb, [n (o) twice, skb] six times, n, o. Row 100: O, k 6, o, k 2, [n (o) twice, n] three times, k 2, o, k 6.
Row 102: O, k 1, o, k 7, o, [n (o) twice, skb] four times, o, k 7. Row 104: O, k 3, o, skb, k 6, o, skb, [n (o) twice, skb] three times, n, o, k 6, n.
Row 106: O, n, o, k 1, (o, skb) twice, k 6, o, skb, k 1, [n (o) twice, skb] twice, k 1, n, o, k 6, n.
Row 108: O, k 2, o, snb, o, k 2, o, skb, k 6, o, skb, k 2, n, (o) twice, skb, k 2, n, o, k 6, n. Row 110: O, k 3, o, snb, o, k 3, o, skb, k 6, o, skb, k 6, n, o, k 6, n. Row 112: O, k 4, o, snb, o, k 4, o skb, k 6, o, skb, n, o, skb, n, o, k 6, n.
Row 114: O, k 5, o, snb, o, k 5, o, skb, k 6, o, skb, k 1, n, o, k 6, n. Row 116: O, k 6, o, snb, o, k 6, o, skb, k 6, o, snb, o, k 6, n. Row 118: O, k 5, n, o, k 3, o, skb, k 5, o, skb, k 13, n. Row 120: O, k 5, n, o, k 5, o, skb, k 5, o, skb, k 11, n.
Row 122: O, k 5, n, o, k 7, o, skb, k 5, o, skb, k 9, n.
Row 124: O, k 7, o, k 3, snb, k 3, o, k 7, o, skb, k 7, n.
Row 126: O, k 8, o, k 3, snb, k 3, o, k 8, o, skb, k 5, n.
Row 128: O, k 9, o, k 3, snb, k 3, o, k 9, o, skb, k 3, n.
Row 130: O, k 8, n, o, k 9, o, skb, k 8, o, skb, k 1, n.
Row 132: K 8, n, o, k 11, o, skb, k 8, o, snb, o. Row 134: k 4, n, k 3, o, k 2, o, skb, k 9, o, k 3, skb, k 4, o, k 3, o.
Row 136: K 3, n, skb, k 2, o, k 3, o, skb, k 8, o, k 2, n, skb, k 3,

o, n, o, k 1, o, skb, o. Row 138: K 2, n, skb, k 2, o, k 4, o, skb, k 7, o, k 2, n, skb, k 2, o, n, o, k 3, o, skb, o. Row 140: K 1, n, skb, k 2, o, k 5, o, skb, k 6, o, k 2, n, skb, k 1, (o, n) twice, o, k 1, (o, skb) twice, o.

Row 142: N, skb, k 2, o, k 6, o, skb, k 5, o, k 2, n, skb, o, (n, o) 2 times, k 3, (o, skb) twice, o, (36 sts in every pattern). Row 144: Snb, k 2, o, k 7, o, skb, k 4, o, k 2, snb, (o, n) three times, o, k 1, (o, skb) three times, o.

Row 146: Snb, k 1, o, k 8, o, skb, k 3, o, k 1, snb (o, n) three times, o, k 3, (o, skb) three times, o. Row 148: Snb, o, k 9, o, skb, k 2, o, snb, (o, n) four times, k 1, (o, skb) four times, o.

Row 150: Skb, o, k 4, n, o, k 1, o, skb, k 4 (o, n) five times, o, k 3, (o, skb) four times, o.

Row 152: K1b, o, k 1, o, skb, k 1, n, o, k 3, o, skb, k 1, n, o, k 1,

o, k1b, (o, n) five times, o, k 1, (o, skb) five times, o.

Row 154: (skb, o) twice, snb, o, n, o, k 1,, o, skb, o, snb, (o, n) seven times, o, k 3, (o, skb) five times, o.

Row 156: O, skb, o, (skb, o) twice, skb, k 1, (n, o) twice, k 1, o, (skb, o) three times, skb, k 1, (n, o) twice, k 1, o, snb, o, k 1, (o, skb) twice, k 1, (n, o) twice, K 1.

Row 158: O, k 3, o (skb, o) twice, snb, (o, n) twice, o, k 3, (o, skb) twice, o, snb, (o, n) twice, o, k 3, (o, skb) twice, o, snb, (o, n) twice.

Row 160: O, k 5, o, skb, o, skb, k 1, n, o, n. Row 162: O, k 7, o, skb, o, snb, o, n.

Row 164: O, k 9, o, skb, k 1, n. Row 166: O, k 11, o, snb.

Row 168: K 13, o, k 1, o.

Row 170: K 5, snb, k 5, o, k 3, o. Row 172: K 4, snb, k 4, o, k 5,

o. Row 174: K 3, snb, k 3, o, k 7, o. Row 176: K 2, snb, k 2, o, k 9, o.

Row 178: K 1, snb, k 1, o, k 11, o. Row 180: O, snb, o, k 13.

Row 182: O, k 3, o, k 5, snb, k 5. Row 184: O, n, o, v 3, o, skb, o, k 4, snb, k 4.

Row 186: (O, n) twice, o, v 3, (o, skb) twice, o, k 3, snb, k 3.

Row 188: (o, n) twice, o, k 5, (o, skb) twice, o, k 2, snb, k 2.

Row 190: (o, n) twice, o, k 7, (o, skb) twice, o, k 1, snb, k 1.

Row 191: K.

Cast off using a crochet hook. Cast off 4 sts at one time, ch 12, cast off 5 sts at one time, ch 12, cast off 4 sts at one time, ch 12, cast off 4 sts at one time, ch 12, cast off 3 sts at one time, ch 12. Continue all around edge. Finished cloth is about 66 inches in diameter.

Place Mats and Napkin Rings

Jute and linen place mats, coasters, and napkin rings add the natural look that is so popular for today's casual dining.

Round Jute Place Mat

Materials
90 yds. 3 ply natural jute
Size K crochet hook

Directions
Ch 6, join with sl st to form a ring.

Rnd 1: Ch 1, make 6 sc in ring, join with sl st to first sc. Rnd 2: Ch 1, 2 sc in each sc around, join. Rnd 3: Ch 1, 2 sc in first sc, 1 sc in next sc, * 2 sc in next sc, 1 sc in next sc. Rep from * around, join.

Rnd 4: Ch 1, * 1 sc in first sc, 1 sc in next sc, 2 sc in next sc. Rep from * around, join. Rnd 5: Same as rnd 3.

Rnd 6: Same as rnd 4. Rnd 7: Ch 1, 1 sc in each of first 4 sc, 2 sc in fifth sc, * 1 sc in each of next 4 sc, 2 sc in fifth sc. Repeat from * around, join. Rnd 8: Ch 1, 1 sc in each sc around, join. Rnd 9: Same as rnd 8. Rnd 10: Same as rnd 7.

Rnd 11: Same as rnd 8. Rnd 12: Same as rnd 8. Rnd 13: Ch 1, 1 sc in each of first 5 sc, 2 sc in sixth sc, * 1 sc in each of next 5 sc, 2 sc in sixth sc. Repeat from * around, join. Rnd 14: Ch 1, 1 sc in each of first 6 sc, 2 sc in 7th sc, * 1 sc in each of next 6 sc, 2 sc in 7th sc. Repeat from * around, join.

Rnd 15 and 16: Same as rnd 8. Fasten off.

Matching Napkin Rings

Materials
6 yds. 3 ply natural jute
Size K crochet hook

continued

Contemporary Place Mats and Napkin Rings *(continued)*

Directions

Ch 10, join with sl st to form a ring.

Rnd 1: Ch 1, 1 sc in each ch st, join. Rnd 2: Ch 1, 1 sc in each sc, join. Rnd 3: Same as rnd 2. Fasten off.

Rectangular Jute Place Mat

Materials

60 yds. 3 ply natural jute
40 yds. 3 ply coral jute
Size K crochet hook

Directions

With natural jute, ch 31.

Row 1: 1 sc in second ch from hook and in each ch to end. Ch 1, turn. Row 2: 1 sc in first and each sc to end. Ch 1, turn. Repeat row 2 for next 24 rows. Fasten off.

Coral Trim—Row 1: 1 sc in each sc starting at right, top edge. 2 sc in same sc at corner and continue down side working 1 sc in between each row. Continue working bottom and other side in same way, ending with sl st to first sc of this row. Row 2: Ch 1, 1 sc in each sc around all four sides, ending with sl st to first sc of this row.

Row 3: * Ch 4, skip 2 sc, 1 sc in next sc. Repeat from * until scalloped on all 4 sides, ending with sl st to first sc of this row. Fasten off. (Skip only 1 sc at corners or wherever needed to make scallops look even.)

Matching Napkin Rings

Materials

6 yds. 3 ply coral jute
Size K crochet hook

Directions

Ch 10, join with sl st to form a ring. Rnd 1: Ch 1, 1 sc in each ch, join with sl st to first sc. Rnd 2: Ch 1, 1 sc in each sc, join. Rnd 3: * Ch 3, sk 1 sc, 1 sc in next sc.

Rep from * until scalloped all the way around, ending ch 3, sk 1 sc, join with sl st to first st in first scallop. Fasten off and turn inside out.

Scallop on other edge same way, keeping scallops directly across from each other.

Coral Coaster

Materials

14 yds. 3 ply coral jute
Size I crochet hook

Directions

Ch 4, join with sl st to form ring. Rnd 1: Ch 1, make 6 sc in ring. Join with sl st to first sc. Rnd 2: Ch 1, 2 sc in each sc around, join. Rnd 3: Ch 1, 2 sc in first sc, 1 sc in next sc, * 2 sc in next sc, 1 sc in next sc, rep from * around, join.

Rnd 4: Ch 1, * 1 sc in first sc, 1 sc in next sc, 2 sc in next sc, repeat from * around, join. Rnd 5: Same as rnd 3. Rnd 6: * Ch 3, skip 2 sc, 1 sc in next sc, repeat from * around, join. Fasten off.

Linen Openwork Place Mat

Materials

½-pound tube, F. J. Fawcett natural (10/2) linen yarn (for two place mats)
Size 8 knitting needles

Gauge

Seed st, 4 sts = 1 inch (blocked)

Directions

In addition to the basic k and p sts, you will need to know how to ksb, which means to k into the st below.

Pattern sts: (10 seed sts used for border not given in directions after pattern begins).

Seed st (even number)—Row 1: K 1, p 1. Row 2: P 1, k 1.

Seed st borders (1st 5 sts and last 5 sts)—Row 1: K 1, p 1, k 1, p 1, k 1, pattern sts, end p 1, k 1, p 1, k 1, p 1. Row 2: K 1, p 1, k 1, p 1, k 1, pattern sts, end p 1, k 1, p 1, k 1, p 1.

Ladder st—Multiple of 5 sts plus 1.

Row 1: * Ksb, k 2 tog, yo, k 2 tog *, rep * to * 13 times, end ksb.

Row 2: * P 2, (k 1, p 1, into yo), p 1 *, rep from * to * 13 times, end p 1.

Cast on 76 sts (after 5 sts put on marker and before last 5 sts. These sts are always seed sts and not included in directions for place mat).

Row 1, 2, 3, 4, 5, 6, 7: Seed st.

Row 8: P the 66 sts bet markers.

Row 9: Begin pat rows 1 and 2, rep 25 times.

Row 59: K across row between markers, being sure to ksb as in previous rows.

Rep 7 rows of seed st. Cast off in pat (this means to con in seed st in cast off row).

Blocking—Dampen mat in medium strength starch and block to size.

Napkin Ring for Linen Place Mat

Materials

Leftover linen from place mats
Size 8 knitting needles

Directions

Cast on 10 sts.

Row 1: K. Row 2: P.

Row 3: * K 2, ksb, k 2 tog, yo, k 2 tog, ksb, k 2.

Row 4: K 2, p 2, k 1, p 1, into yo, p 2, k 2. Rep rows 3 and 4 four times. K 4 rows *. Rep from * to * 3 times. *Note:* Always ksb on 3rd and 8th sts.

Cast off and sew two ends tog.

Blocking—Dip napking ring in full strength starch and slip it onto any bottle that measures six inches in circumference. Dry, then remove napkin ring.

Spiral Crocheted Table Toppers

Once you've mastered this basic pattern, you can make lots of different size mats for your table. An entire luncheon set of this tasteful design will go well with several different-style table settings. Here, you see a touch of the old fashioned combined with a natural contemporary look. You may also use this tasteful pattern for much more elegant dining. Or if you like, make a single doily or a set of small coasters as a charming gift.

Materials

J. & P. Coats "Knit Cro-Sheen" Amount determined by size and number of doilies
Size 7 steel crochet hook

Directions

Note: Place mat measures 17¼ inches in diameter; next size, 7½ inches in diameter; next size, 4¾ inches in diameter; smallest size, 4¼ inches in diameter.

Ch 5, join with sl st to form a ring.

Rnd 1: * ch 4, sc in ring, rep from * 5 more times (6 loops on this rnd). Hereafter, do not join rnds.

Rnd 2: * ch 4, 2 sc in loop, rep from * around.

Rnd 3: * ch 4, 2 sc in loop, sc in next sc, rep from * around.

Rep rnd 3 until desired size, then * ch 4, sc in loop, ch 4, sk first sc, sc in each sc skipping the last sc, rep from * around.

Continue in this manner, hav-

ing 2 less sc in each sc group and 1 loop more bet sc groups in each rnd, until 1 sc remains in each sc group. End last rnd with ch 2, dc in first sc to form last loop.

If the piece seems to need extra sts to allow it to lie flat, increase the amount of sts in the ch between the sc groups.

Continue as described until the doily has attained the desired size.

When groups of loops meet, fasten off thread. Steam press doily to block.

MEASURING WORK

Spread your knit or crochet articles out on a flat surface without stretching them. Measure down the center.

When you are measuring the length, always place a marker, such as a safety pin or piece of colored thread, in the center of the row so that the measurement from that point will be accurate.

Country-style Crocheted Place Mats

For a quick and easy crochet project that's bound to attract rave notices, try these flower place mats. Made of washable rug yarn, they're no problem when it's time to launder them.

Materials

Coats & Clark's Craft and Rug Yarn, 140 yd. pull-out skeins
  3 cocoa brown
  2 ivory
  2 dk. brown
Size I crochet hook
Note: The above material will make 5 mats, each 17 inches in diameter.

Directions

First flower—Starting at center with cocoa brown, ch 8. Join with sl st to form ring. Rnd 1: Ch 1, * sc in ring, ch 3, then, holding back on hook the last loop of each tr, make 2 tr in same ring, yo hook and draw through all 3 lps on hook—cluster made; ch 3. Rep from * 5 times. Join with sl st to first sc—6 petals. Fasten off. Mark first flower as center flower.

Second flower—With cocoa brown, ch 8. Join to form ring. Rnd 1: Ch 1, in ring make sc, ch 3 and cluster, with wrong side of first flower facing, join with sl st to top of any petal on first flower, ch 3. Rep from * on first rnd of first flower. Fasten off.

Third flower—With cocoa brown, ch 8. Join. Rnd 1: Ch 1, in ring make sc, ch 3 and cluster, with wrong side facing, join to top of next free petal on first flower to the right of previous joining of petals; ch 3, in same ring make sc, ch 3 and cluster, join to top of next free petal on second flower, ch 3 and com-

plete flower as before. Make and join 3 more flowers as third flower was joined to first and second flowers.

Seventh flower—Work as before until first and second petals have been joined; work 3 more petals; then make another petal joining it to corresponding petals on first and second flowers.

Border—Attach ivory to any joining sl st between petals on outer edge of center. Rnd 1: Ch 1, sc in same place where yarn was attached, * (ch 5, sc in top of next cluster) 3 times; ch 5, sc in joining sl st between next 2 petals. Rep from * around. Join last ch 5 to first sc—24 lps. Rnd 2: Ch 1, 5 sc in each lp around. Join to first sc. Fasten off.

Attach dark brown to center sc on any lp. Rnd 3: Ch 1, sc in same place where yarn was attached, * ch 5, sc in center sc on next loop. Rep from * around. Join. Rnd 4: Ch 1, sc in same place as sl st, * 5 sc in next lp, sc in next sc. Rep from * around. Join.

Rnd 5: Sl st in next 2 sc, ch 1, sc in next sc, ch 6, sk next 5 sc, sc in next sc. Rep from * around. Join. Rnd 6: Ch 5, in same place as sl st make tr, ch 1 and tr, * ch 1, tr in next lp, ch 1, in next sc make (tr, ch 1) twice and tr. Rep from * around. Join to fourth ch of ch 5. Fasten off.

Attach ivory to center tr of any 3 tr group. Rnd 7: Ch 1, sc where yarn was attached, * ch 3, sk next tr, sc in next tr, ch 3, sc in center tr of next 3 tr group. Rep from * around. Join. Rnd 8: Ch 1, 3 sc in each lp around. Join. Ch 1, turn and work sl st loosely in each sc. Join to first sl st. Fasten off.

With rust-proof pins, pin mat out to measurement and steam lightly through damp cloth. Allow to dry thoroughly before removing pins so it will retain blocked measurement.

For Your Bedroom

What could add more beauty and character to a bedroom than a handmade crocheted or knitted bedspread, an assortment of pillows, or even a coverlet for a baby's bassinet or crib? Comfort and an air of relaxation are of prime importance in furnishing and decorating bedrooms, and these lovely patterns convey that message. You will find traditional, contemporary, and country styles. And by adding or deleting a few stitches, you can adapt them to fit any bed size. Instructions for the bed cover and pillows shown here are given on pages 38-39.

Knitted Bed Cover and Pillows (shown on pages 36-37)

Our beautifully patterned bed cover snugs a mattress like a contour sheet. It measures 39x75x7½ inches thick and fits a single bed mattress.

Key pillows to drawings. Ssk means slip 2 sts knitwise, and k the two tog.

Knitted Bed Cover

Materials

Coats & Clark "Speed-Cro-Sheen"
  35 balls brown
Size 5 36-inch-long circular knitting needle
4 yds. ¼-inch-wide elastic

Gauge

19 sts = 4 inches, 13 rows = 2 inches

Directions

Top—Starting at the lower edge, cast on 185 sts; do not join. Turn. Starting with a p row; work 4 rows in stockinette stitch (p 1 row, k 1 row).

Work pat as follows—Row 1: (wrong side) p across.

Row 2: K 3, * yo, with yarn in back sl 1 as if to p, k 1, psso, k 7, k 2 tog, yo, k 1. Rep from * across, end last rep with yo, k 3. Row 3 and all wrong-side rows: p across.

Row 4: K 4, * yo, sl 1, k 1, psso, k 5, k 2 tog, yo, k 3. Rep from * across, end last rep with yo, k 4. Row 6: K 3, * (yo, sl 1, k 1, psso) twice; k 3, (k 2 tog, yo) twice; k 1. Rep from * across, end last rep with k 3. Row 8: K 4, * (yo, sl 1, k 1, psso) twice; k 1, (k 2 tog, yo) twice; k 3.

Rep from * across, end last rep with k 4. Row 10: K 3, * (yo, sl 1, k 1, psso) twice; yo, sl 1, k 2 tog, psso, yo, (k 2 tog, yo) twice; k 1. Rep from * across, end last rep with k 3.

Row 12: Rep row 8. Row 14: K 5, * yo, sl 1, k 1, psso, yo, sl 1, k 2 tog, psso, yo, k 2 tog, yo, k 5. Rep from * across. Row 16: K 6, * yo, sl 1, k 1, psso, k 1, k 2 tog, yo, k 7. Rep from * across, end last rep with k 6. Row 18: K 7, * yo, sl 1, k 2 tog, psso, yo, k 9. Rep from * across, end last rep with yo, k 7. Rows 20, 22, and 24: K across. Row 25: P across.

Rep these 24 rows (rows 2 through 25) for pattern until total length is about 72 inches, ending with row 23. Bind off.

Note: Two or three inches are allowed for stretching when blocking.

Side—Cast on 42 sts. Row 1: K 2 for casing, sl 1 as if to k for turning ridge of casing; k 39. Row 2: P across. Rep these two rows alternately until total length is about 216 inches, without stretching. Bind off. Stretch side to measure about 225 inches when blocking.

Finishing—Block to measurements. Sew short edges of side piece tog. Turn casing to wrong side at turning ridge and stitch in place, leaving a 1-inch opening for elastic. Sew opposite long edge of side to outer edge of top with seam at a corner, and easing in outer edge of top to fit. Slip elastic through casing; pull to desired length and cut elastic, allowing 1 inch for sewing. Sew ends of elastic together; sew across opening.

Small Ecru Pillow (No. 1)

Materials

Cotton parcel post twine
  300 yds.
Size 6 knitting needles
½ yd. lining fabric
Thread
1 lb. Dacron/polyester stuffing

Gauge

9 sts = 2 inches, 7 rows = 1 inch

Directions

Pillow front—Cast on 52 sts.
  Row 1: (wrong side) p.
  Row 2: K 2, * yo, k 2 tog, k 4, ssk, yo, k 2; rep from *. *Note:* Ssk, means to slip 2 stitches knitwise, then knit the 2 sts tog. Rep rows 1 and 2 (pat) until 12 inches from beginning. Bind off all sts. Make back same as front.

Finishing—Block each piece to a 12-inch square (string will stretch slightly when pillow is stuffed): Sew three sides together. Cut two pieces of fabric 13½ inches square and with right sides together, stitch on three sides (½-inch seams). Turn lining right side out, press, stuff, and slip-stitch fourth side closed. Insert pillow in knitted cover; stitch fourth side of cover closed.

Natural Jute Pillow (No. 2)

Materials

4 ply jute
  2 balls natural
Size 10½ knitting needles
½ yd. lining fabric
Thread
Dacron/polyester pillow stuffing

Gauge

3 sts = 1 inch, 3 rows = 1 inch

Directions

Pillow front—Cast on 42 sts. Follow pat (rows 1 and 2) given for small ecru pillow above. Continue pat until 14 inches from beg. Bind off. Make back same as front.

Finishing—Block both pieces to measure 14x17 inches. Sew three sides together. Cut two pieces of fabric 15½x18½ inches for lining. Stitch together on three sides, turn to right side, press, and stuff. Stitch fourth side closed. Insert lining in pillow cover; stitch fourth side of cover closed.

Natural String
Pillow (No. 3)

Materials
Parcel post twine, 160 yd. balls
  4 balls
Size 10 knitting needles
½ yd. lining fabric
Thread
Dacron/polyester pillow stuffing
Sewing needle

Gauge
3 sts = 1 inch, 4 rows = 1 inch

Directions
Pillow front—Working with two
strands of string together, cast
on 48 sts. Rows 1 and 2: P.
  Row 3 (wrong side): K.
  Row 4: * k 1, (yo, ssk) 3 times,
k 1; rep from *.
  Rows 5, 7, 9, 11: P.

  Rows 6, 10: * k 2, (yo, ssk) 2
times, k 2; rep from *.
  Row 8: * k 3, yo, ssk, k 3; repeat from *.
  Row 12: Rep row 4.
  For pat, rep rows 1 to 12 four
more times. Rep rows 1 to 3
once. Bind off. Make back the
same.
  Finishing—Block pieces to
measure 14x16 inches. Stitch
tog on three sides. Cut two pieces
of fabric 15½x17½ inches. Stitch
together on three sides, turn,
press, stuff, and stitch fourth side
closed. Insert pillow form; stitch
fourth side closed.

Spice-Colored
Pillow (No. 4)

Materials
Coats & Clark "Speed-Cro-
Sheen"

4 balls spice
Size 8 knitting needles
½ yd. lining fabric
Thread
Dacron/polyester pillow stuffing

Gauge
4 sts = 1 inch, 6 rows = 1 inch

Directions
Front and back—Working with
two strands together, cast on 40
sts. Then, follow instructions for
working front and back of natural string pillow (No. 3) above.
  Finishing—Block both pieces
to 12x11 inches. Stitch three
sides together. Cut two pieces
of fabric 13½x14½, stitch together on three sides. Turn,
press, stuff, and stitch fourth side
closed. Insert pillow form in
cover; sew fourth side of pillow
closed.

Filet-Patterned Bed Coverlet (or Tablecloth)

This old and treasured pattern has just as much appeal today as it ever did. To crochet a spread this size, you need twenty 10½-inch-square blocks. Or alter the dimensions to fit any bed (or table).

Materials
Bedspread Crochet Cotton, 650 yd. balls
 8 balls white
Size 5 steel crochet hook

Gauge
Each square approximately 10½ x10½ inches without edging

Directions
Ch 8, join with sl st to form a ring.

Row 1: Ch 3 (counts as first dc), make 3 more dc in ring, * ch 5, 4 dc in ring, rep from * around twice more, ending with ch 5, sl st in top of first dc.

Row 2: Ch 3 (counts as first dc), dc in next 3 dc (3 dc in next sp, ch 5, 3 dc in same sp)—makes corner sp—dc in next 4 dc, 3 dc in next sp, ch 5, 3 dc in same sp, dc in next 4 dc, 3 dc in next sp, ch 5, 3 dc in same sp, dc in next 4 dc, 3 dc in next sp, ch 5, 3 dc in same sp, sl st in top of first dc.

Row 3: Ch 5, sk 2 dc, dc in next dc, ch 2, sk 2 dc, dc in next dc, * ch 2, dc in center st of next ch 5 sp, ch 5, dc in same sp, ch 2, dc in next dc, ch 2, sk 2 dc, dc in next dc, ch 2, sk 2 dc, dc in next dc, ch 2, sk 2 dc, dc in next dc, rep from * twice more. End with ch 2; join with sl st in third st of starting ch.

Row 4: Ch 5, dc in next dc, ch 2, dc in next dc, 2 dc in next sp, dc in next dc, 3 dc in next sp, ch 5, 3 dc in same sp, dc in next dc, * 2 dc in next sp, dc in next dc, (ch 2, dc in next dc) 3 times, 2 dc in next sp, dc in next dc (3 dc, ch 5, 3 dc) in corner sp, rep from * twice more. Then dc in next dc, 2 dc in next sp, ch 2, sl st in third st of starting ch.

Row 5: Ch 5, dc in next dc, 2 dc in next sp, dc in next 7 dc * (3 dc, ch 5, 3 dc) in next sp, dc in next 7 dc, 2 dc in next sp, dc in next dc, ch 2, dc in next dc, 2 dc in next sp, dc in next 7 dc, rep from * twice more, ending with 2 dc in next sp, sl st in top of first dc.

Row 6: Ch 5, dc in next dc (ch 2, sk 2 dc, dc in next dc) 4 times, * ch 2, dc in center st of next sp, ch 5, dc in same sp as last dc, ch 2, dc in next dc (ch 2, sk 2 dc, dc in next dc) 4 times, ch 2, dc in next dc (ch 2, sk 2 dc, dc in next dc) 4 times, rep from * once more, ending with ch 2, sl st in third st of starting ch.

Row 7: Ch 5, dc in next dc (ch 2, dc in next dc) 3 times, (2 dc in next sp, dc in next dc) 2 times, 3 dc, ch 5, 3 dc in next sp (corner sp), * dc in next dc (2 dc in next sp, dc in next dc) twice, (ch 2, dc in next dc) 7 times, (2 dc in next sp, dc in next dc) twice, (3 dc, ch 5, 3 dc) in next sp, rep from * twice more. Then (dc in next dc, 2 dc in next sp) twice, dc in next dc, ch 2, dc in next dc, ch 2, dc in next dc, ch 2, sl st in third st of starting ch.

Row 8: Ch 5, dc in next dc (ch 2, dc in next dc) twice, 2 dc in next sp, dc in next 10 dc's, (3 dc, ch 5, 3 dc), corner sp, * dc in next 10 dc, 2 dc in next sp, dc in next dc (ch 2, dc in next dc) 5 times, 2 dc in next sp, dc in next 10 dc's, (3 dc, ch 5, 3 dc), corner sp, rep

continued

Filet-Patterned Bedspread *(continued)*

from * twice more, ending with dc in next 10 dc, 2 dc in next sp, dc in next dc, ch 2, dc in next dc, ch 2, sl st in third st of starting ch.

Row 9: Ch 5, dc in next dc (ch 2, dc in next dc) twice, (ch 2, sk 2 dc, dc in next dc) 5 times, ch 2, dc in third st of corner ch, ch 5, dc in same sp as last dc, ch 2, dc in next dc, * (ch 2, sk 2 dc, dc in next dc) 5 times, (ch 2, dc in next dc) 5 times, (ch 2, sk 2 dc, dc in next dc) 5 times, ch 2, dc in third st of corner ch, ch 5, dc in same sp as last dc, ch 2, dc in next dc, rep from * twice more, ending with (ch 2, sk 2 dc, dc in next dc) 5 times, ch 2, dc in next dc, ch 2, sl st in third st of ch.

Row 10: Ch 5, dc in next dc, (ch 2, dc in next sp) 5 times * (2 dc in next sp, dc in next dc) 3 times, in corner sp make 3 dc, ch 5, 3 dc, dc in next dc, (2 dc in next sp, dc in next dc) 3 times, (ch 2, dc in next dc) 11 times, rep from * 3 more times ending with (ch 2, dc in next dc) 4 times, ch 2, sl st in third st of starting ch.

Row 11: Ch 5, dc in next dc (ch 2, dc in next dc) 4 times, 2 dc in next sp, dc in next 13 dc, in corner sp make 3 dc, ch 5, 3 dc, * dc in next 13 dc, 2 dc in next sp, dc in next dc (ch 2, dc in next dc) 9 times, 2 dc in next sp, dc in next 13 dc, in corner sp make 3 dc, ch 5, 3 dc, rep from * three more times, ending with dc in next 13 dc, 2 dc in next sp, dc in next dc, (ch 2, dc in next dc) 3 times, ch 2, sl st in third st of ch.

Row 12: Ch 5, dc in next dc, (ch 2, sk 2 dc, dc in next dc) 6 times, * ch 2, dc in third st of corner sp, ch 5, dc in same sp as last dc, ch 2, dc in next dc, (ch 2, sk next 2 dc, dc in next dc) 6 times, (ch 2, dc in next dc) 9 times, (ch 2, sk next 2 dc, dc in next dc) 6 times, rep from * twice more, ending with (ch 2, dc in next dc) 3 times, ch 2, sl st in third st of starting ch.

Row 13: Ch 3, 2 dc in next sp,

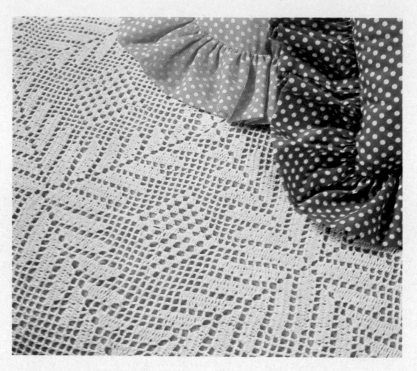

dc in next dc, (ch 2, dc in next dc) 7 times, * 2 dc in next sp, (dc in next dc) 4 times, in corner sp make 3 dc, ch 5, 3 dc, (dc in next dc, 2 dc in next sp) 4 times, (ch 2, dc in next dc) 7 times, 2 dc in next sp, dc in next dc, (ch 2, dc in next dc) 7 times, rep from * three more times, (dc in next dc, 2 dc in next sp) 4 times, (ch 2, dc in next dc) 6 times, ending with ch 2, sl st in top of first dc.

Row 14: Ch 5, sk next 2 dc, dc in next dc, 2 dc in next sp, dc in next dc (ch 2, dc in next dc) 5 times, * 2 dc in next sp, dc in next 16 dc, in corner sp make 3 dc, ch 5, 3 dc, dc in next 16 dc, 2 dc in next sp, dc in next dc, (ch 2, dc in next dc) 5 times, 2 dc in next sp, dc in next dc, ch 2, sk 2 dc, dc in next dc, 2 dc in next sp, dc in next dc, (ch 2, dc in next dc) 5 times, rep from * twice more, ending with 2 dc in next sp, dc in next 16 dc, in corner sp make 3 dc, ch 5, 3 dc, dc in next 16 dc, 2 dc in next sp, dc in next dc (ch

2, dc in next dc) 5 times, ch 2, sl st in third st of ch.

Row 15: Ch 3, 2 dc in next sp, dc in next dc, ch 2, sk next 2 dc, dc in next dc, 2 dc in next sp, dc in next dc (ch 2, dc in next dc) 4 times, (ch 2, sk 2 dc, dc in next dc) 7 times, ch 2, dc in center st of next sp, ch 5, dc in same sp, ch 2, dc in next dc, * (ch 2, sk next 2 dc, dc in next dc) 7 times, (ch 2, dc in next dc) 4 times, 2 dc in next sp, dc in next dc, ch 2, sk next 2 dc, dc in next dc, 2 dc in next sp, dc in next dc, ch 2, sk 2 dc, dc in next dc, 2 dc in next sp, dc in next dc, (ch 2, dc in next dc) 4 times, (ch 2, sk 2 dc, dc in next dc) 7 times, ch 2, dc in center st of next sp, ch 5, dc in same st, ch 2, dc in next dc, rep from * twice more, ending with (ch 2, sk 2 dc, dc in next dc) 7 times, (ch 2, dc in next dc) 4 times, 2 dc in next sp, dc in next dc, ch 2, sl st in top of first dc.

Row 16: Ch 5, sk 2 dc, dc in next dc, 2 dc in next sp, dc in next dc, ch 2, sk 2 dc, dc in next dc, 2 dc in next sp, dc in next dc, (ch 2, dc in next dc) 6 times, (2 dc in next sp, dc in next dc) 5 times, in corner sp make 3 dc, ch 5, 3 dc, dc in next dc, * (2 dc in next sp, dc in next dc) 5 times, (ch 2, dc in next dc) 6 times, 2 dc in next sp, dc in next dc, ch 2, sk 2 dc, dc in next dc, 2 dc in next sp, dc in next dc, ch 2, sk 2 dc, dc in next dc, 2 dc in next sp, dc in next dc, (ch 2, dc in next dc) 6 times, (2 dc in next sp, dc in next dc) 5 times, in corner sp make 3 dc, ch 5, 3 dc, dc in next dc, rep from * twice more, ending with (2 dc in next sp, dc in next dc) 5 times, (ch 2, dc in next dc) 6 times, 2 dc in next sp, dc in next dc, ch 2, sk 2 dc, dc in next dc, 2 dc in next sp, sl st in top of first dc.

Row 17: Ch 3 (counts as first dc), 2 dc in next sp, dc in next dc, ch 2, sk 2 dc, dc in next dc, 2 dc in next sp, dc in next dc, ch 2, sk 2 dc, dc in next dc, 2 dc in next sp, dc in next dc (ch 2, dc in next dc) 4 times, dc in next dc, 2 dc in next sp, dc in next 19 dc, in corner sp make 3 dc, ch 5, * dc in next 19 dc, 2 dc in next sp, dc in next dc, (ch 2, dc in next dc) 4 times, (2 dc in next sp, dc in next dc, ch 2, sk next 2 dc, dc in next dc) 4 times, 2 dc in next sp, dc in next dc, sk 2 dc, dc in next dc, 2 dc in next sp, dc in next dc, sk 2 dc, dc in next dc, 2 dc in next sp, dc in next dc, sk 2 dc, dc in next dc, 2 dc in next sp, dc in next dc, (ch 2, dc in next dc) 4 times, 2 dc in next sp, dc in next 19 dc, in corner sp make 3 dc, ch 5, 3 dc, rep from * twice more, ending with dc in next 19 dc, 2 dc in next sp, dc in next dc (ch 2, dc in next dc) 4 times, 2 dc in next sp, dc in next dc, ch 2, sk 2 dc, dc in next dc, 2 dc in next sp, dc in next dc, ch 2, sl st in top of first dc.

Row 18: Ch 5, dc in next dc, 2 dc in next sp, dc in next dc, ch 2,

sk 2 dc, dc in next dc, 2 dc in next sp, dc in next dc, ch 2, sk 2 dc, dc in next dc, 2 dc in next sp, dc in next dc, ch 2, sk 2 dc, dc in next dc, 2 dc in next sp, dc in next dc (ch 2, dc in next dc) 3 times, (ch 2, sk 2 dc, dc in next dc) 8 times, ch 2, dc in center st of corner, ch 5, dc in same st, ch 2, dc in next dc, * (ch 2, sk 2 dc, dc in next dc) 8 times, (ch 2, dc in next dc) 3 times, (2 dc in next sp, dc in next dc, sk next 2 dc, dc in next dc) 5 times, 2 dc in next sp, dc in next dc (ch 2, dc in next dc) 3 times, (ch 2, sk 2 dc, dc in next dc) 8 times, ch 2, dc in center st of corner sp, ch 5, dc in same st, rep from * twice more, ending with (ch 2, sk 2 dc, dc in next dc) 8 times, (ch 2, dc in next dc) 3 times, 2 dc in next sp, dc in next dc, ch 2, sk 2 dc, dc in next dc, 2 dc in next sp, dc in next dc, ch 2, sk 2 dc, dc in next dc, 2 dc in next sp, sl st in third st of ch.

Row 19: Ch 3, 2 dc in next sp, dc in next dc (ch 2, sk 2 dc, dc in next dc, 2 dc in next sp, dc in next dc) 3 times, (ch 2, dc in next dc) 5 times, (2 dc in next sp, dc in next dc) 6 times, in corner sp make 3 dc, ch 5, 3 dc, * dc in next dc, (2 dc in next sp, dc in next dc) 6 times, (ch 2, dc in next dc) 5 times, (2 dc in next sp, dc in next dc, ch 2, sk 2 dc, dc in next dc) 6 times, 2 dc in next sp, dc in next dc, (ch 2, dc in next dc) 5 times, (2 dc in next sp, dc in next dc) 6 times, in corner sp make 3 dc, ch 5, 3 dc, rep from * twice more, ending with (2 dc in next sp, dc in next dc) 6 times, (ch 2, dc in next dc) 5 times, 2 dc in next sp, dc in next dc, ch 2, sk 2 dc, dc in next dc, 2 dc in next sp, dc in next dc, ch 2, sl st in top of first dc.

Joining blocks—Sew all blocks together with a whipstitch, being careful to match stitches. See photo at the left.

Edging—Row 1: Attach thread in any corner sp, ch 3 (counts

as first dc), dc in same sp, ch 2, sk 2 dc, dc in next 2 dc, ch 2, sk 2 dc, dc in next 2 dc. Con in this manner, evenly spacing 2 dc around. In the corners make 2 dc, ch 5, 2 dc. End rnd by making 1 dc, ch 5 in beg corner, make sl st in top of first dc.

Row 2: Ch 3 (counts as first dc), dc in same sp, ch 3, 2 dc in next sp, ch 3, 2 dc in next sp. Continue in this manner until corner sp, then make 2 dc, ch 5, 2 dc, in next sp make 2 dc, ch 3, 2 dc. Continue on around work ending with ch 5, sl st in top of first dc.

Row 3: Rep row 2.

Row 4: Ch 3 (counts as first dc), ch 1, dc in same sp, ch 1, dc in same sp, ch 1, dc in same sp, ch 1, dc in same sp (this makes 5 dc with ch 1 sp bet) in corner sp, then ch 3, sk next 3 sp, in next ch 3 sp make (dc, ch 1) 5 times. Continue in pattern. In each corner sp, make (dc, ch 1) 5 times. End rnd with sl st in top of first dc.

Row 5: Sl st to first sp bet dc's, ch 5, sl st in first st of ch making a picot, sc in next sp, ch 5, picot, sc in next sp, ch 5, picot, sc in next sp, ch 3, sc in next sp, ch 3, sc in sp bet dc's, ch 5, picot. Continue on in pattern, ending with ch 3, sl st in first st.

Colonial-Style Knitted Bedspread

Enduring charm—and a style that never loses its loveliness—are two of the wonderful features of this antique reproduction. What's more, you can enjoy the benefits of museum-like quality, with none of the drawbacks, because our 80x100-inch knitted spread is made of washable acrylic yarn.

Materials
Bernat Berella "4," 4 oz. balls
    40 off-white
Size 8 knitting needles

Gauge
Each square should measure 10 inches. One ball of Bernat Berella "4" will make 2 squares.
Note: Always slip as if to purl.

Directions
Square—Make 80. Cast on 1 st. Inc rows—Row 1: K, inc 1 st in same st. Row 2: K 1, k, inc 1 st in next st. Row 3: K 2, k, inc 1 st in last st. Row 4: K 3, k, inc 1 st in last st. Rows 5 through 22: K to last st, k, inc 1 st in same st—23 sts.

Row 23: P to last st, p, inc 1 st in same st. Row 24: K 1, * k 2 tog, k 1, yo, rep from * to last 2 sts, k 1, k, inc 1 st in last st. Row 25: P to last st, p, inc 1 st in same st.

Rows 26 through 34: K to last st, k, inc 1 st in same st. Row 35: P to last st, p, inc 1 st in same st. Row 36: K 1, * k 2 tog, k 1, yo, rep from * to last 2 sts, k 1, k, inc 1 st in last st. Row 37: Rep row 25:

Rows 38 through 41: K to last st, k, inc 1 st in same st. Row 42: K 3, yo, k 1, yo, * k 6, yo, k 1, yo, rep from * to last 3 sts, k 2, k, inc 1 st in last st.

Row 43: K 4, p 3, * k 6, p 3, rep from * to last 3 sts, k 2, k, inc 1 st in last st. Row 44: K 4, yo, k 3, yo, * k 6, yo, k 3, yo, rep from * to last 4 sts, k 3, k, inc 1 st in last st.

Row 45: K 5, p 5, * k 6, p 5, rep from * to last 4 sts, k 3, k, inc 1 st in last st. Row 46: K 5, yo, k 5, yo, * k 6, yo, k 5, yo, rep from * to last 5 sts, k 4, k, inc 1 st in last st. Row 47: * k 6, p 7, rep from * to last 5 sts, k 4, k, inc 1 st in last st.

Row 48: K 6, * sl 1, k 1, psso, k 3, k 2 tog, k 6, rep from * to last 6 sts, k 5 instead of k 6, k, inc 1 st in last st.

Row 49: K 7, * p 5, k 6, rep from * to last 6 sts, k 5 instead of k 6, k, inc 1 st in last st. Row 50: K 7, * sl 1, k 1, psso, k 1, k 2 tog, k 6, rep from * to last st, k, inc 1 st in same st.

Row 51: K 8, * p 3, k 6, rep from * to last st, k, inc 1 st in same st. Row 52: K 8, * k 3 tog, k 6, rep from * to last 2 sts, k 1, k, inc 1 st in last st. Rows 53 through 56: K to last st, k, inc 1 st in same st.

Rows 57 and 59: P to last st, p, inc 1 st in same st. Rows 58, 60, and 61: K to last st, k, inc 1 st in same st—62 sts.

Dec rows—Row 1: K to last 3 sts, k 2 tog, k 1. Row 2: P to last 3 sts, p 2 tog, p 1. Row 3: K to last 3 sts, k 2 tog, k 1. Row 4: Rep row 2.

Rows 5 through 13: Rep row 3. Row 14: P to last 3 sts, p 2 tog, p 1. Row 15: K 1, * k 2 tog, k 1, yo, rep from * to last 2 sts, k 2 tog—47 sts.

Row 16: P to last 3 sts, p 2 tog, p 1. Row 17: K to last 3 sts, k 2 tog, k 1. Row 18: Rep row 16. Row 19: K 1, * k 2 tog, k 1, yo, rep from * to last 4 sts, k 1, k 2 tog, k 1—43 sts.

Row 20: P to last 3 sts, p 2 tog, p 1. Rows 21 through 29: K to last 3 sts, k 2 tog, k 1. Rows 30, 32, and 34: P to last 3 sts, p 2 tog, p 1. Rows 31, 33, 35, and 36: K to last 3 sts, k 2 tog, k 1.

Row 37: K 12, yo, k 1, yo, k to last 3 sts, k 2 tog, k 1—27 sts. Row 38: K 12, p 3, k to last 3 sts, k 2 tog, k 1. Row 39: K 11, yo, k 3, yo, k to last 3 sts, k 2 tog, k 1.

Row 40: K 11, p 5, k to last 3 sts, k 2 tog, k 1. Row 41: K 10, yo, k 5, yo, k to last 3 sts, k 2 tog, k 1. Row 42: K 10, p 7, k to last 3 sts, k 2 tog, k 1. Row 43: K 9, yo, k 7, yo, k to last 3 sts, k 2 tog, k 1.

Row 44: K 9, p 9, k to last 3 sts, k 2 tog, k 1. Row 45: K 8, yo, k 9, yo, k to last 3 sts, k 2 tog, k 1. Row 46: K 8, p 11, k to last 3 sts, k 2 tog, k 1.

Row 47: K 7, sl 1, k 1, psso, k 7, k 2 tog, k to last 3 sts, k 2 tog, k 1. Row 48: K 7, p 9, k to last 3 sts, k 2 tog, k 1. Row 49: K 6, sl 1, k 1, psso, k 5, k 2 tog, k to last 3 sts, k 2 tog, k 1.

Row 50: K 6, p 7, k to last 3 sts, k 2 tog, k 1. Row 51: K 5, sl 1, k 1, psso, k 3, k 2 tog, k to last 3 sts, k 2 tog, k 1. Row 52: K 5, p 5, k to last 3 sts, k 2 tog, k 1. Row 53: K 4, sl 1, k 1, psso, k 1, k 2 tog, k to last 3 sts, k 2 tog, k 1.

Row 54: K 4, p 3, k to last 3 sts, k 2 tog, k 1. Row 55: K 3, k 3 tog, k to last 3 sts, k 2 tog, k 1. Rows 56 through 59: K to last 3 sts, k 2 tog, k 1. Row 60: K 2 tog, k 1. Row 61: K 2 tog. Fasten off.

Finishing—Referring to photograph, with right side facing you and matching rows, sew 4 squares tog to form a block. Sew 5 blocks tog to form a strip. Sew 4 strips tog to complete coverlet.

Fringe—Cut strands of yarn 17 inches long. Knot 5 strands in every other st around 2 long edges and 1 short end of coverlet. Trim ends. Steam lightly.

Crocheted Bed Canopy or Valance

Remember when your favorite linen hankies were trimmed with dainty hand-crocheted edgings? If so, you'll be amazed to know that this bold bed canopy was made from just such an old-fashioned edging pattern. Executed in natural jute, it makes a world of difference.

Why not experiment with expanding the scope of old crochet patterns in new ways like this? Besides using this pattern for a bed canopy, use it also to make dramatic valances to add the finishing touch to simple window treatments.

Materials

4 ply jute (amount determined by length of valance)
Size J crochet hook
Note: Scallops are 20 inches deep and 16 inches across. Experiment with various weights of cord, string, or jute, and with different sizes of crochet hooks to get a valance that is in scale with your particular needs.

Directions

Ch 17. Row 1: Dc in fourth ch from hook, 1 dc in next ch, in next ch make cluster, ch 2, cluster, (to make cluster: make 3 dc in same sp, holding back last loop of each, thread over and through all loops at once), ch 2, sk 2 ch, cluster in next ch, ch 2, dc in last ch.

Row 2: Ch 3, turn; make cluster with the turning ch counting as first dc and 2 dc in next sp, ch 2, cluster in next sp, ch 2, (cluster, ch 2, cluster) in ch 2 sp between previous clusters, dc in next dc, ch 3, dc in each of next 3 dc, dc in turning ch.

Row 3: Ch 3, turn; dc in each of next 3 dc, ch 3, dc in next dc, (cluster, ch 2, cluster) in center of previous double cluster, ch 2, cluster in next sp, ch 2, cluster in next sp, ch 2, cluster in turning ch.

Row 4: Ch 3, turn; sk first sp, cluster in next sp, ch 2, cluster in next sp, ch 2 (cluster, ch 2, cluster) in center of previous double cluster, dc in next dc, ch 3, dc in each of next 3 dc and in turning ch.

Row 5: Ch 3, turn; dc in each of next 3 dc, ch 3, dc in next dc, (cluster, ch 2, cluster) in center sp of previous double clusters, ch 2, cluster in next sp, dc in top of next cluster.

Row 6: Ch 3, turn; sk first sp, in center of previous double clusters make (cluster, ch 2, cluster), dc in next dc, ch 3, dc in each of next 3 dc, dc in turning ch.

Row 7: Ch 3, turn; dc in each of next 3 dc, ch 3, dc in next dc, in center of previous double clusters make (cluster, ch 2, cluster) ch 2, cluster in next sp, ch 2, dc in turning ch of previous row.

Ch 3, turn; go back and rep from row 2 for pat, until reaching desired length. End work with row 2.

Edging—(Do not cut jute) Ch 5, turn, sc in top of fourth dc, ch 5, sc in next sp, ch 5, sc in next sp, ch 5, sc in next sp, etc. Continue on in this manner having ch 5 loops around bottom of work. When you get to the end, ch 1, turn work around, make 8 sc in each loop around. At end, sl st in last sc and cut jute.

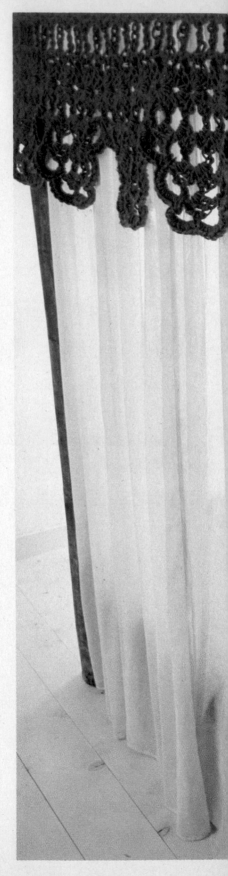

Crib Coverlets

A handmade coverlet for a baby's crib, carriage, or bassinet is surely a labor of love. Whether it's for your own baby—or a gift for someone else's—you'll delight in trying these easy-to-stitch patterns.

Coverlet on Chair

Materials
Columbia-Minerva Nantuk Bulky, 2 oz. skeins
    2 green (A)
    2 lt. green (B)
    2 yellow (C)
    2 orange (D)
    2 peach (E)
    2 pink (F)
Size K crochet hook

Gauge
1 pat (13 sts) = 4½ inches; 1 row = 1 inch

Directions
With A, ch 87 to measure approximately 32 inches.

Row 1: Dc in 3rd ch from hook (ch 2 always counts as first dc), dc in each of next 2 ch, (sk 1 ch, dc in each of next 5 ch, 3 dc in next ch, dc in each of next 5 ch, sk 1 ch) 6 times, dc in each of last 3 ch, working off last 2 loops of last dc with B, cut A. Ch 2, turn.

Row 2: Sk first dc, through *back loops* only dc in each of next 2 dc, (sk 1 dc, dc in each of next 5 dc, 3 dc in next dc, dc in next 5 dc, sk 1 dc) 6 times, dc in each of last 3 dc, working off last 2 loops of last dc with C, cut B. Ch 2, turn.

Row 3: Working through *front loops* only rep row 2, working off last 2 loops of last dc with D, cut C, ch 2, turn.

Row 4: Rep row 2, working off last 2 loops of last dc with E, cut D, ch 2, turn.

Row 5: Rep row 3, working off last 2 loops of last dc with F, cut E, ch 2, turn.

Row 6: Rep row 2, working off last 2 loops of last dc with A.

Continue in color sequence and pat (ridge is always on same side) until there is a total of 37 color stripes, ending with A stripe. Do not fasten off. Secure all ends, matching color stripes. Edging—Rnd 1: Ch 1, turn. Through *back loops* only, work sl st loosely in each dc to corner, 2 sc in each row to lower edge, sl st in each ch (base of dc) to corner, 2 sc in each row to top edge. Join and fasten off. Join A in first sc on side edge. From same side as first rnd, work sl st loosely in each sc on edge. Join and fasten off. Work sl st in same way on other side. Steam lightly.

Coverlet on Bassinet

Materials
Coats & Clark Craft and Rug Yarn, 4 oz. skeins
    2 white
    2 lime green
    3 yellow
Size H aluminum crochet hook

Gauge
Each square measures 3¾ inches

Directions
Make 15 squares, using lime for the 1st rnd, yellow for 2nd rnd, and white for 3rd rnd. Make 20 squares, using white for the 1st rnd, lime for 2nd rnd, and yellow for 3rd rnd.

Basic square—With 1st color ch 4; join with sl st to form a ring. Rnd 1: Ch 3 (counts as 1 dc) 2 dc in center of ring, * ch 3, 3 dc in center of ring, rep from * 2 more times, end with ch 3; join with sl st to top of ch 3. End off.

Rnd 2: With 2nd color, in ch 3 sp of previous rnd work (ch 3, 2 dc, ch 3, 3 dc) corner, * in next ch 3 sp work (3 dc, ch 3, 3 dc), rep from * twice, join with sl st to top of ch 3. End off.

Rnd 3: With 3rd color, (ch 3, 2 dc, ch 3, 3 dc) in ch 3 at corner sp, then work 3 dc between each 3 dc group on sides and (3 dc, ch 3, 3 dc) in each corner; join with sl st. End off.

Assembling—Arrange the blocks with the 15 blocks that have lime for the 1st rnd in three rows with five blocks in each row. Use the 20 squares that have white for the 1st rnd to make a border rectangular center section. Whipstitch together on wrong side, picking up top back loops only.

Border—Row 1: With yellow work 3 dc between groups of dc along all edges, and (3 dc, ch 3, 3 dc) in each corner. End off.

Rows 2, 3, 4, and 5: Repeat as for row 1, alternating with lime and white rows.

Note: To make picot, ch 3, sl st in first ch. Row 6: Attach yellow to ch 3 corner, (ch 3, 2 dc, ch 3, picot, 3 dc) in same sp, * picot, 3 dc between next group of dc, repeat from * along all edges, and (3 dc, picot, 3 dc) in each corner; join with sl st to top of ch 3. End off.

LEFTOVER YARN

■ *You can use leftover yarns for many projects. Just be sure that it's all the same weight and fiber.*
■ *You can also use fine yarns, if you combine two or more strands with heavier yarns, such as knitting worsted. (Work a small sample to see exactly how many strands produce the same weight.)*
■ *Test the yarn for color fastness before combining it with other colors. Wash a small amount, and if the water becomes discolored, don't mix it with other yarns.*

Embroidered Knitted Throw

This white throw, with sprigs of wildflowers embroidered on large triangles, adds a lift to either an adult's or a child's room.

Knit of alternate triangles of garter stitch and stockinette stitch, it measures 38x50 inches.

Materials

Knitting worsted, 4 oz. skeins
   5 white
Persian or Persian-type yarn,
3 ply, 1 oz. skeins
   4 bright yellow
   1 lt. yellow
   5 lavender-pink
   5 bright green
   1 lt. green
   5 medium blue
Size 8 knitting needles
Size K crochet hook
Blunt-end tapestry needle

Gauge

4 sts = 1 inch
Note: Make six 12x18-inch st st triangles, six 12x18-inch garter st triangles, four 12x9-inch st st triangles, and four 12x9-inch garter st triangles (see page 52).

Directions

12x18-inch st st triangles—cast on 72 sts. Row 1: p. Row 2: k 2 tog, k to last 2 sts, k 2 tog. Rep rows 1 and 2 until 1 st remains. Break yarn and draw end through rem st.

12x18-inch garter st triangles —cast on 72 sts. Row 1: k. Row 2: k 2 tog, k to last 2 sts, k 2 tog. Rep rows 1 and 2 until 1 st remains. Break yarn and draw end through rem st.

12x9-inch st st triangles—cast on 36 sts. Row 1: p. Row 2: k 2 tog, k to end of row (no dec at end of row). Rep rows 1 and 2 until 1 st remains. Break yarn and draw the end of the yarn through rem st. Make two triangles like this, two with the dec at the end of the k rows instead of at the beginning.

12x9-inch garter st triangles— cast on 36 sts. Row 1: k. Row 2: k 2 tog, k to end of row (no dec at end of row). Rep rows 1 and 2 until 1 st remains. Break yarn and draw end of yarn through rem st. Make two triangles like this, 2 with the dec at the end of the dec row instead of at the beg.

Press triangles lightly with steam iron, and embroider floral motifs on the six large st st triangles. Arrange triangles (see drawing) and whipstitch all of the sections together.

Crochet border—Row 1: Sc all around afghan. Row 2: Sc 2 sts, dc 4 sts in 1st st, * skip 2 sts, dc 5 sts in 3rd st. Rep from * around row. Fasten off.

Embroidery—*Note:* Work the flowers, stems, and leaves freehand on the blanket, following a basic pattern. Use a double strand of yarn throughout. Work thread ends into the back to avoid knots.

Step 1: First, embroider circular flowers in Pekinese stitch (see diagrams) in each of the 12x18-inch st st triangles. For this stitch, work a framework of straight stitches and then lace yarn through the framework to form flower "petals." Don't pull the yarn too tightly as you work; it should stand slightly above the surface of the knitting. Each triangle has a large flower and a small one.

On one end of the blanket, work the larger flower in yellow and the smaller one in pink; then reverse the colors for the opposite end. Work light green French knots in the center of the yellow flowers and light yellow French knots in the center of the pink flowers.

Step 2: Add gently curving stems in stem stitch to the yel-low and pink flowers. Work leaf stems in stem stitch and leaves in individual chain stitches.

Step 3: Finally, add a sprinkling of four or five blue forget-me-nots with bright yellow centers to each triangle to balance the larger flowers and stems. Make the forget-me-nots with five petals in individual chain stitches around a French knot.

Pekinese stitch

1. Work a foundation of small running stitches from A to B in a spiral shape:

2. Then, starting at B, Work running stitches back along the spiral, filling in the blank spaces left the first time. Bring the thread up again at A.

3. From here on out, the needle does not enter the knit background. Slip the needle from the bottom up under stitch number 2 and pull thread through.

4. Bring the needle back and under the first stitch, from the top down. Carry the needle *over* the working thread and pull it through.

5. Begin the next stitch by carrying the needle under stitch number 3, from the bottom up.

continued

Embroidered Knitted Throw *(continued)*

6. Pull thread through and insert the needle under stitch number 2, from the top down, and over the working thread.

7. Continue working this way, as in steps 5 and 6, to the end of the line.

Crocheted Bed Throw

For something out of the ordinary, use this crocheted throw to top a patchwork quilt, and let the bright colors peek through the cobweb-like designs of the coverlet.

Materials
4 ply sportweight yarn, 2 oz. skeins, ivory or eggshell
   61 (for twin-size bed)
   83 (for queen-size bed)
Size F crochet hook

Gauge
Each finished square should measure about 5¼ inches across. *Note:* Make 27 squares for twin-size bed, 33 for queen-size bed.

Directions
To begin: Ch 10 and join into ring with sl st.

Rnd 1: Ch 3, (counts as first dc); make 31 dc in ring; join with a sl st to first dc of rnd.

Rnd 2: Ch 3; dc bet each dc of preceding rnd (inserting hook under all 3 yarns bet each st of preceding rnd); join with a sl st to first ch 3 of rnd.

Rnd 3: Ch 3; * crochet 1 dc bet each dc of preceding rnd; 7 times (making first of these 7 dc just after sl st at end of preceding rnd, and again being sure to insert hook under all 3 yarns); crochet 2 dc in next st (first corner) *; rep from * to * 2 more times. Finish rnd with 8 dc; join with a sl st.

Rnd 4: Ch 3; * crochet 8 dc, then 1 dc in first corner st of preceding rnd (inserting hook under all 3 yarns in middle of dc); 1 ch, 1 dc in second corner st. * Repeat 2 more times from * to *, beg in sp bet corner dc and following dc. Finish fourth side with 8 dc, 1 dc in corner dc, ch 1, and join with a sl st.

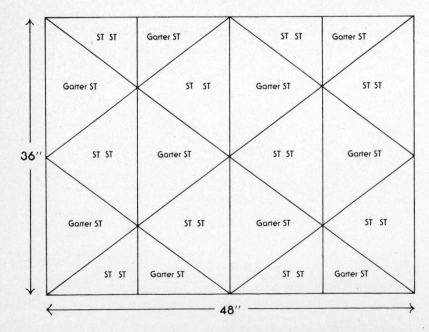

Rnd 5: Ch 3; * 9 dc, then crochet 1 dc in first dc of corner, ch 3, 1 dc in other corner dc *. Rep 2 more times from * to *. Finish rnd with 9 dc, 1 dc in corner dc, ch 3, join with a sl st.

Rnd 6: Ch 3; * dc 10, crochet 1 dc in first dc of corner, ch 5, dc 1 in other corner dc *. Rep 2 more times from * to *. Finish rnd with 10 dc, 1 dc in corner dc, ch 5; join with sl st.

Rnd 7: Ch 3; * dc 11, dc 1 in corner dc, ch 7, dc 1 in other corner dc *. Rep from * to * 2 more times. Finish rnd with 11 dc, 1 dc in corner dc, ch 7, and join with a sl st.

Rnd 8: Ch 3; * dc 12, dc 1 in first dc of corner, ch 9, dc 1 in other corner dc *. Rep 2 more times from * to *. Finish off square with 12 dc, 1 dc in first dc of corner, ch 9, 1 sl st; break yarn and pull through last st, being sure to leave about 24 inches of yarn with which to join squares.

Joining—To join first 27 (33) squares: Iron squares on wrong side, using damp cloth. Arrange in "L" shape with 17 squares on long side, and 10 on shorter side (19 and 15 for queen-size bed).

Note: Now is the time to measure your bed to see if you'll need additional squares for length or width. With squares still arranged in an L-shape, join dc sides (not ch sts) using sl st on wrong side.

Finishing—To complete the spread: Now make 160 (252) squares as follows: For each of the next 160 (252) squares, follow directions for the first 7 rnds. On the 8th rnd, join each square to the L-framework as follows: Proceed with first three sides of eighth rnd as above, but finish the fourth side with 12 dc, 1 dc in corner dc, ch 7, then 1 sl st in the middle of ch 9 of the square directly above, ch 3, 1 sl st in the middle of ch 9 of square directly to left, ch 3, 1 sl st in 4th ch st of square you are finishing up, ch 3, and then 1 sl st to close the square. Now join dc sides of new square to the dc sides of adjacent squares, using sl st on the wrong side (as for joining initial squares into L-shape above).

Continue to join squares, as each is completed, to the framework of original squares, using the L-framework as top and side edges of the spread.

Handcrafted Rugs

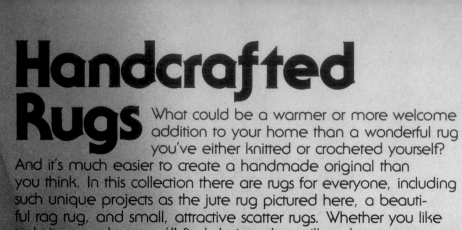

What could be a warmer or more welcome addition to your home than a wonderful rug you've either knitted or crocheted yourself? And it's much easier to create a handmade original than you think. In this collection there are rugs for everyone, including such unique projects as the jute rug pictured here, a beautiful rag rug, and small, attractive scatter rugs. Whether you like to knit or crochet, you'll find designs that will make your fingers itch to get started. Materials vary from the jute used to make the contemporary rug below (see page 56 for instructions) to the conventional types of rug yarns and even recycled materials such as old clothes, blankets, or sheets cut into narrow strips and joined together.

Crocheted Jute Rug *(shown on pages 54-55)*

Unbleached raw jute is a rugged material that you'll be able to transform into a beautiful, durable area rug that will be a natural for many decorating schemes.

You only need to know a few simple crochet stitches to make this rug composed of textured 12-inch squares. To join the crocheted squares, use the drawing at the right as a guide for arranging them in parquet pattern.

Materials
Unbleached 3 ply jute (amount required depends on the size of rug you wish to make and how tightly you crochet. Work up a sample square and calculate your needs accordingly).
Size J crochet hook
Note: The rug pictured consists of 26 sc squares, 27 dc squares, and 27 squares of alternating rows of sc and dc sts—80 patches in all, each measuring approximately 12 inches square.

Because you are working with raw jute, the yarn will vary in width and bulkiness; hence, there might be a slight difference in the size of each square. Correct this by stretching and blocking to uniform size before joining.

Measurements for blocking
Finished rug is slightly larger than 8x10 feet after scalloped edge is added to the rug ends.

Directions
Sc square: With size J crochet hook, ch 22. Row 1: Sc in second ch from hook, sc in each ch (21 sts per row). Rep until you have 16 rows. Make 27 squares.

Dc square: Ch 23. Row 1: Dc in third ch from hook, dc in each ch (21 sts per row). Rep until you have 8 rows. Make 27 squares.

S/dc square: Ch 22. Row 1: Sc in second ch from hook, sc in each ch (21 sts per row). Row 2: Ch 2, work dc in each st. Row 3: Ch 1, work 1 sc in each st. Rep rows 2 and 3 until you have 6 rows of sc and 5 rows of dc. Make 26 squares.

Finish squares by cutting the two ends of string and, using crochet hook, tuck both ends under three or four sts. Tuck both ends under on same side of square (wrong side of rug).

Before you sew the squares together, lay them out in parquet pattern, as illustrated in our diagram. Arrange the squares in 10 rows of 8 squares each, alternating among the 3 patterns (single, double, and single/double), and alternating the directions of each square.

Join the squares together, using a ch st. To avoid numerous bulky loose ends, join two squares together and then, with-out cutting the yarn, move on to the next two squares. Continue until you have joined 8 pairs of squares in a row. Weave the end of the yarn back into the rug (on the wrong side). Next, join a row of 8 more squares to the original set of 8 pairs. Proceed until all squares are joined horizontally.

Finally, join the squares along the vertical rows. Clip the ends of yarn and use crochet hook to work loose ends back into the wrong side of the rug.

To finish the rug, circle the entire rug with a row of sc, making 3 sc in one st at each corner of the rug. Add another row of sc at one end of rug (side with 8 squares). Ch 1, turn and start scalloped edge. Sc in first sc, * dc in fourth st (center of scallop), dc five more times in same st (6 dc in scallop). Sc in seventh st. * Rep between *'s until you have scallops all along one end (about 28). Rep procedure for scallop trim on opposite end of rug.

Gently steam-press rug.

Patchwork Accent Rug

You'll enjoy this knit project because it's so quick and easy. Knit every row (garter stitch), using double strands of rug yarn and large needles. Mixing a combination of deep tones with one lighter color produces an interesting "crayoned" effect.

Materials

Heavy-duty rug yarn, 70 yd.
skeins
   32 off-white
    4 cerise
    6 yellow
    5 chartreuse
   17 turquoise
Size 11 knitting needles
Tapestry needle

Measurements for blocking

Approximately 4½x6½ feet.

Directions

Note: Use double strands of yarn. For each 12-inch square, cast on 29 sts. Use one strand of off-white and one of a color. Work in garter st (k every row) until piece measures 12 inches. (Each square requires one full skein each of white and a color.) Bind off. Make 15 squares.

For the 9-inch-wide borders, cast on 21 sts. Use one strand of off-white and one of turquoise. (The short sides require about 3½ skeins each of white and turquoise, the long sides about 5 skeins of each.) Work in garter st. Make two strips 36 inches long and two strips 78 inches long.

Using a tapestry needle and a double strand of rug yarn, join the squares together, arranging the colors in a pleasing design, such as the one shown below. Attach the border strips to the center section in same manner.

58

Crocheted Rag Rug

Here's an ideal project
for the beginning
crocheter. Once you learn
how to make the very
basic chain and a single
crochet stitch, this
new fashion variation of
the old-style hit-and-
miss rag rug is a snap.
You'll find every step
and stitch illustrated in
the easy-to-follow
diagrams on the following
pages. To color-
scheme a rug, as was done
with the blue and
white one shown here,
you'll need a well-
stocked rag bag of old
clothes, fabric scraps,
and remnants all in the
same color family.
Look for solids, prints,
plaids, and checks
to combine so the overall
effect will be one
of many tints and shades.

continued

Crocheted Rag Rug *(continued)*

Materials

Approximately 9 yards of 45-inch fabric (or the equivalent in salvaged materials) is needed to make a circular rug 3 to 4 feet in diameter. (One yard of 45-inch fabric, sheet weight, will yield about 44 yards of 1-inch strips, including seam allowance.)
Size J crochet hook
Soil repellent coating
Note: The rug shown here is about 8 feet in diameter and has been worked in blue and white fabrics.

Directions

Collect your rags by cutting old clothes, worn sheets, and other fabrics that are either all-cotton or cotton blends. To color-scheme a rug like this one, select a good mix of solid colors, patterns, prints, and checks.

Cut or tear the fabric into strips between ¾ and 1½ inches wide, depending on the weight of your fabric. For example, tear a heavyweight fabric such as denim into ¾-inch strips; a medium-weight fabric such as sheeting into one-inch strips; and light-weight cotton into 1½-inch sections. All strips of any given fabric should be the same width.

Join the strips together into a workable length by machine-stitching the strips together on the diagonal as shown in Diagram 1. Trim the seam allowances. When you've created long "strings" of fabric strips, roll them into a ball like the ones piled in the laundry basket in the picture above.

Using a size J crochet hook, ch six sts (Diagram 2), and join them into a ring with a sl st (Diagram 3). Now, in the first st of ring do a sc st (Diagram 4, Steps A-E). When completed, do another sc in the same st (an inc —

Diagram 5). Rep in all six sts of the ring.

Thereafter, continue sc (Diagram 4); inc in every other st for the second row, and thereafter as necessary in order to maintain the rug's circular shape and flatness. To change colors or add new strips, join a new strip to the preceding one by hand (stitch two pieces together along the diagonal, as before, and clip the seam). Continue working in sc, increasing occasionally and changing colors as you choose, until the rug is the desired size.

To finish the rug, cut the last three or four yards of fabric strips narrower (decreasing to about ⅜ inch wide at the end) so that the last round of the rug will decrease in width, allowing you to end smoothly.

Finally, spray the rug with a soil repellent. To clean rug, launder in a heavy-duty machine.

RUGMAKING TIPS

■ *You may use a variety of fabrics for making crocheted rag rugs. All-cotton, cotton blends, wools, polyesters, and nylon (including hosiery) are all excellent materials. Be sure, however, to use only one fabric type in a rug.*

■ *If you make a rug larger than 3x5 feet, plan to use a pad beneath it. This ensures a longer life and makes your rug easier to vacuum.*

■ *For small rugs, use non-skid padding underneath or sew rubber jar rings to the four corners of the rug.*

■ *To store handmade rugs, roll rather than fold them.*

■ *Clean large handmade rugs the same way you would commercially made rugs—either professionally or with a rug cleaner.*

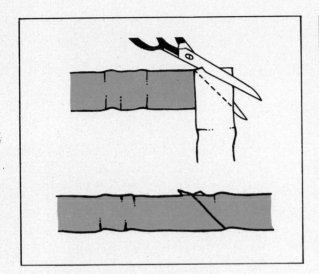

1 Join strips of fabric together on the diagonal. Trim seam.

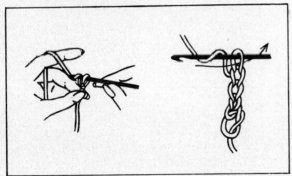

2 Crochet a chain of six stitches.

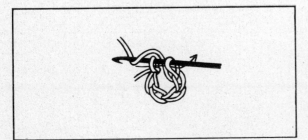

3 Join chain into a ring with a slip stitch.

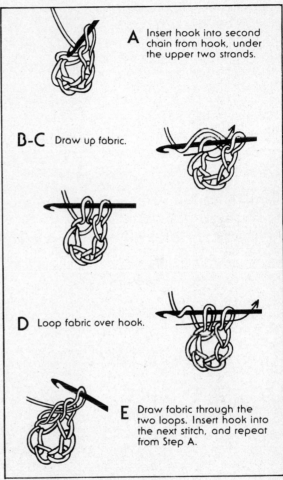

A Insert hook into second chain from hook, under the upper two strands.

B-C Draw up fabric.

D Loop fabric over hook.

E Draw fabric through the two loops. Insert hook into the next stitch, and repeat from Step A.

4 Work entire rug, using a single crochet stitch (see steps above).

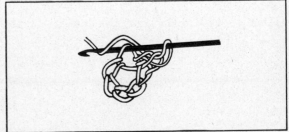

5 To increase, do two stitches (Diagram 4, A-E) in one loop.

Shaker Design Crocheted Rug

Although the colors in this crocheted rug are more vivid than those used long ago in Shaker communities, the style itself is an adaptation of a classic design.

The rug measures approximately 60x100 inches, a size that lends itself well to a family room or an informal living room. It's made of rug yarn, but if you have a rag bag that's bulging with old garments and leftover fabrics, you may decide to make this same pattern with fabric.

continued

Shaker Design Crocheted Rug *(continued)*

Materials

Rayon and cotton rug yarn, 70-yard skeins

18 white
9 turquoise icing
9 peacock
9 sea blue
9 lt. jade
6 lt. yellow
6 lt. avocado
6 black
6 chartreuse
6 evergreen
6 antique gold
6 wood brown

Large tapestry needle
⅝-inch diameter wood or plastic crochet hook

Note: Use three strands of each color throughout entire rug. A parenthesis followed by a number means that you repeat the instructions within the parentheses the specified number of times.

Directions

Center—Using sea blue, ch 5, sl st to 1st ch to make a ring. Row 1: Ch 3, 11 dc in ring, sl st into 3rd ch, break off. (12 st counting ch 3) Row 2: Turquoise icing: sl st in one st, ch 2, dc same st, 2 dc in each of next 7 sts, cut yarn; tie in light jade in back of last st, 2 dc next 4 sts, sl st 2nd ch, end. (24 sts)

Row 3: White: sl st in any st, ch 2, 1 dc in same st, 1 dc in next st, (2 dc next st, 1 dc) around, sl st in 2nd ch, end.

Row 4: Light yellow: sl st in 2nd st back, ch 2, dc in same st, 1 dc in next 2 st, (2 dc tog, 1 dc in next 2 st) 6; tie on antique gold (2 dc tog, 1 dc in next 2 st) 5, sl st 2nd ch, end.

Row 5: Light avocado: sk 6 sts, sl st, ch 2, dc in same st, 1 dc in next 3 sts, (2 dc tog, 3 dc) 5; tie on chartreuse, (2 dc tog, 3 dc) 6, sl st 2nd ch, end. Row 6: Peacock: sk 4 sts, sl st, ch 2, dc in same st, 1 dc in next 4 sts, (2 dc tog, 4 dc)

7; tie on turquoise ice, (2 dc tog, 4 dc) 4, sl st to 2nd ch, end.

Row 7: Sea blue: sl st in 14th st back, ch 2, dc in same st, 1 dc in next 5 sts, (2 dc tog, 5 dc) 8; Tie on evergreen, (2 dc tog, 5 dc) 3, sl st to ch 2, end. Row 8: White: sl st, ch 2, dc in same st, 1 dc in next 6 sts, (2 dc tog, 6 dc) around, sl st 2nd ch, end.

Row 9: Peacock: sl st in 8th st back, ch 2, dc in same st, 1 dc in next 7 sts, (2 dc tog, 7 dc) 3; tie on light jade, (2 dc tog, 7 dc) 8, sl st 2nd ch, end. Row 10: Black: sk 15 sts, sl st, ch 2, dc in same st, 1 dc in next 8 sts, (2 dc tog, 8 dc) 4; tie on wood brown, (2 dc tog, 8 dc) 7, sl st to 2nd ch, end.

Row 11: White: sl st, ch 2, dc in same st, 1 dc in next 9 sts, (2 dc tog, 9 dc) around, sl st to 2nd ch, end. Row 12: Antique gold: sk 4 sts, sl st, ch 2, dc in same st, 1 dc in next 10 sts, (2 dc tog, 10 dc) 6; tie on light yellow, (2 dc tog, 10 dc) 5, sl st to 2nd ch, end.

Row 13: Light jade: sl st in 2nd st back, ch 2, dc in same st, 1 dc in next 11 sts, (2 dc tog, 11 dc) 4; tie on light avocado, (2 dc tog, 11 dc) 7, sl st to 2nd ch, end. Row 14: Turquoise ice: sk 16 sts, sl st, ch 2, dc in same st, 1 dc in next 12 sts, (2 dc tog, 12 dc) 7; tie on peacock, (2 dc tog, 12 dc) 4, sl st to 2nd ch, end.

Row 15: White: sl st, ch 2, dc in same st, 1 dc in next 13 sts, (2 dc tog, 13 dc) around, sl st to 2nd ch, end.

First Side—Row 16: Chartreuse: sl st in 2 sts, sc in 2 sts, hdc, 2 dc in next st, 1 dc in next 9 sts, (2 dc tog, 14 dc) 2; tie on light yellow, 2 dc tog, 14 dc, 2 dc tog, 9 dc, hdc, 2 sc, 2 sl sts, end. (80 sts) Row 17: Sea blue: sk 5 sts at beg of row 16, sl st next st, 1 sc in next 2 sts, hdc, dc, 2 dc tog, 13 dc, 2 dc tog, 1 dc in next 14 sts, 2 dc tog, 7 dc; tie on light avocado, 7 dc, 2 dc tog, 13 dc, 2 dc tog, dc, hdc, 2 sc, sl st, end.

Row 18: White: sk 5 sts at beg

of row 17, sl st, sc, hdc, dc in next 2 sts, (2 dc tog, 14 dc) 3, 2 dc tog, 8 dc, 2 dc tog, 2 dc, hdc, sc, sl st, end. (70 sts). Row 19: Turquoise ice: sk 4 sts, sl st, sc, hdc, 2 dc, (2 dc tog, 14 dc) 2; tie on peacock, 2 dc tog, 14 dc, 2 dc tog, 5 dc, 2 dc tog, 2 dc, hdc, sc, sl st, end.

Row 20: Light jade: sk 3 sts at beg of row 19, sl st, sc, hdc, 2 dc, 2 dc tog, 10 dc, 2 dc tog, 12 dc; tie on sea blue, (2 dc tog, 12 dc) 2, 2 dc tog, 2 dc, hdc, sc, sl st, end. Row 21: Wood brown: sk 3 sts at beg of row 20, sl st, sc, hdc, 2 dc, 2 dc tog, 9 dc, (2 dc tog, 12 dc) 2; tie on black, 2 dc tog, 12 dc, 2 dc tog, 2 dc, hdc, sc, sl st, end.

Row 22: Light avocado: sk 3 sts at beg of row 21, sl st, sc, hdc, 2 dc, 2 dc tog, 8 dc, 2 dc tog, 12 dc; tie on turquoise ice, (2 dc tog, 12 dc) 2, 2 dc tog, 2 dc, hdc, sc, sl st, end. Row 23: White: sk 2 sts at beg of row 22, sl st, sc, hdc, 2 dc, 2 dc tog, 15 dc, 2 dc tog, 16 dc, 2 dc tog, 15 dc, 2 dc tog, 2 dc, hdc, sc, sl st, end. Row 24: Light yellow: sk 2 sts at beg of row 23, sl st, sc, hdc, 2 dc, 2 dc tog, 15 dc, 2 dc tog, 16 dc; tie on antique gold, 2 dc tog, 15 dc, 2 dc, hdc, sc, sl st, end.

Row 25: Sea blue: sk 2 sts at beg of row 24, sl st, sc, hdc, 2 dc, 2 dc tog, 15 dc, 2 dc tog, 8 dc; tie on peacock, 8 dc, 2 dc tog, 15 dc, 2 dc tog, 2 dc, hdc, sc, sl st, end. Row 26: White: rep row 23.

Second Side—Row 16: Light yellow: on row 15 sk 15 sts from end of row 16, 2 sl st, 2 sc, hdc, 2 dc tog, 9 dc, (2 dc tog, 14 dc) 2; tie on antique gold, 2 dc tog, 14 dc, 2 dc tog, 9 dc, hdc, 2 sc, 2 sl st, end. Row 17: Chartreuse: sk 5 sts at beg of above row, sl st, 2 sc, hdc, dc, 2 dc tog, 14 dc; tie on sea blue, (2 dc tog, 14 dc) 2, 2 dc tog, 13 dc, dc, hdc, 2 sc, sl st, end.

Row 18: Same as for first side. Row 19: Peacock: sk 4 sts at beg of above row, sl st, sc, hdc, 2 dc, (2 dc tog, 14 dc) 2; tie on light jade, 2 dc tog, 14 dc, 2 dc tog, 5 dc, 2 dc tog, 2 dc, hdc, sc, sl st, end. Row 20: Turquoise ice: sk 3 sts at beg of above row, sl st, sc, hdc, 2 dc, 2 dc tog, 10 dc, (2 dc tog, 12 dc) 3, 2 dc tog, 2 dc, hdc, sc, sl st, end.

Row 21. Evergreen: sk 3 sts at beg of row 20, sl st, sc, hdc, 2 dc, 2 dc tog, 9 dc, 2 dc tog, 12 dc, 2 dc tog, 6 dc; tie on black, 6 dc, 2 dc tog, 12 dc, 2 dc tog, 2 dc, hdc, sc, sl st, end. Row 22: Light avocado: sk 3 sts at beg of row 21, sl st, sc, hdc, 2 dc, 2 dc tog, 8 dc, (2 dc tog, 12 dc) 2; tie on chartreuse, 2 dc tog, 12 dc, 2 dc tog, 2 dc, hdc, sc, sl st, end.

Row 23: Same as for first side. Row 24: Chartreuse: sk 2 sts from beg of row 23, sl st, sc, hdc, 2 dc, 2 dc tog, 15 dc; tie on light yellow, 2 dc tog, 16 dc, 2 dc tog, 15 dc, 2 dc tog, 2 dc, hdc, sc, sl st, end.

Row 25: Sea blue: sk 2 sts at beg of row 24, sl st, sc, hdc, 2 dc, 2 dc tog, 15 dc, 2 dc tog, 16 dc; tie on peacock, 2 dc tog, 15 dc, 2 dc tog, 2 dc, hdc, sc, sl st, end. Row 26: Same as for first side.

Corners (first side, right corner)—Row 27: Turquoise ice: sk 2 sts from beg of row 26 (first side), sl st, sc, hdc, 2 dc, 2 dc tog, 10 dc, 2 hdc, 2 sc, 2 sl st, end. Row 28: Black: sk 2 sts at beg of row 27, sl st, sc, hdc, dc, 2 dc tog, 6 dc, 2 hdc, 2 sc, sl st, end. Row 29: Peacock: sk 2 sts at beg of row 28, sl st, sc, hdc, 3 dc, 3 dc, 2 dc tog, 2 dc, hdc, 2 sc, sl st, end.

First side, left corner—Row 27: Turquoise ice: on row 26, following row 27, right corner, sk 16 sts, 2 sl st, 2 sc, 2 hdc, 10 dc, 2 dc tog, 2 dc, hdc, sc, sl st, end. Row 28: Evergreen: sk 5 sts at beg of above row, sl st, 2 sc, 2 hdc, 6 dc, 2 dc tog, dc, hdc, sc, sl st, end. Row 29: Sea blue: sk 4 sts at beg of above row, sl st, 2 sc, hdc, 2 dc, 2 dc tog, 3 dc tog,

hdc, sc, sl st, end.

Corners (second side)—Repeat above directions, using following colors: Right corner—Row 27: turquoise ice. Row 28: evergreen. Row 29: light jade. Left corner—Row 27: turquoise ice. Row 28: black. Row 29: sea blue.

Border—Begin in 2nd of 3 dc tog in right corner of first side. Row 1: Light yellow: sl st, ch 2, 4 dc in same corner st, dc across to next corner, 5 dc in corner st, 19 dc; tie on chartreuse, 52 dc; antique gold, dc to corner, 5 dc in corner, 16 dc; light yellow, dc to corner, 5 dc in corner, 10 dc; chartreuse, 60 dc; antique gold, dc to end, sl st to join in 2nd ch, end.

Row 2: Light avocado, sk 1 st, sl st, ch 2, 4 dc in corner st, 17 dc; chartreuse, dc to corner; light jade, 5 dc in corner, 32 dc; turquoise ice, 13 dc; light avocado, dc to corner; light jade, 5 dc in corner, 33 dc; light avocado, dc to corner; turquoise ice, 5 dc in corner, 38 dc; light jade, 17 dc; turquoise ice, 23 dc; light avocado, dc to end, sl st, end.

Row 3: White: dc around with 5 dc in each corner. Row 4: Peacock, sk 1 st, sl st, ch 2, 4 dc in corner st, 45 dc; sea blue, dc to corner, 5 dc in corner st, 32 dc; peacock, 32 dc; turquoise ice, dc to corner; sea blue, 5 dc in corner, dc to next corner, 5 dc in corner, 27 dc; peacock, 46 dc; light jade, dc to end, sl st to ch 2, end.

Row 5: Turquoise ice, sk 1 st, sl st, ch 2, 4 dc in corner st, 35 dc; light jade, dc to corner; peacock, 5 dc in corner, 17 dc; turquoise ice, 25 dc; sea blue, 32 dc; peacock, dc to corner, 5 dc in corner, dc to next corner; light jade, 5 dc in corner, 18 dc; light avocado, 27 dc; sea blue, 49 dc; turquoise ice, dc to end, sl st to ch 2, end.

Row 6: Evergreen, sk 1 st, sl

st, ch 2, 4 dc in corner st, 14 dc; black, dc to corner, 5 dc in corner, 10 dc; wood brown, 43 dc; evergreen, dc to corner; black, 5 dc in corner, 25 dc; wood brown, 21 dc; evergreen, dc to corner, 5 dc in corner, 35 dc; wood brown, 14 dc; black, 42 dc; evergreen, dc to end, sl st to ch 2, end.

Weave in ends with tapestry needle; trim. Block with steam iron. Do not press.

RECYCLING YARNS

Don't indiscriminately discard outmoded hand knitted or crocheted projects.
■ Examine the yarn—and if it's still in good condition plan to salvage for reuse in other projects. Here's how: First unravel the yarn, winding it into a large skein. Now, hold end of yarn between thumb and forefinger and wind around elbow and back between thumb and forefinger. Continue until skein is about the size of a skein of knitting worsted. Next, lay it out flat and tie a strand of yarn loosely around skein in several places. (This prevents yarn from tangling).
■ To unkink yarn, immerse in water until it is completely saturated, wrap in a Turkish towel, and squeeze out excess moisture. Stretch skein over back of a chair and let it dry completely. If yarn is not unkinked, repeat process.

Easy-To-Stitch Scatter Rugs

Small rugs can add instant beauty to almost any room. And these, one knitted and one crocheted, are made of washable rug yarn. The knitted checkerboard design has a contemporary air, while the crocheted rug, with its familiar zigzag pattern, is reminiscent of days gone by. The knitted rug measures 29x36 inches; the crocheted rug can, however, be made any size you wish.

Knit Rug (left in photo)

Materials
Aunt Lydia's Rug Yarn, 70 yd. skeins
  7 burnt orange
  7 navy
Size 10½ circular knitting needle
Size I aluminum crochet hook
10 ring markers

Gauge
3 sts = 1 inch on one side (6 sts of double knit)

Directions
Pattern—Double knit with one color as a practice before starting with two colors.
Note: In addition to the basic knitting stitches, you will need to know yf (bring yarn forward), yb (take yarn to back), and pso (pass stitch over).

Row 1: * k 1 (yf), s 1 (pw) *, rep * to * every row. (This gives st face.) Row 2: * k 1, (yb). s 1 (pw), * rep * to * every row. (This gives garter stitch face.)

As an exercise, you can make a potholder by casting on 42 sts, dividing into units of 14 sts each. Work row 1 for 14 sts, row 2 for 14 sts, and row 1 for 14 sts, * rep * to * to desired size.

Double knit with two colors: Group No. 1 (1st side).

Block No. 1 (blue st face.)—A; * k 1 navy, (yf): P 1 orange (yb) *, rep for 18 sts, slip ring to right needle, take navy (yb), orange (yf).

Block No. 2 (orange garter st face)—B: * p 1 orange, k 1 navy *, rep from * to * for 14 sts, slip ring to right needle, orange (yb).

No. 1 (2nd side)

Block No. 1 (orange st face)—C: * k 1 orange (yf), p 1 navy (b) *, rep from * to * for 18 sts, navy (yf), orange (yb).

Block No. 2 (navy garter st face)—D: * p 1 blue, k 1 orange, * rep from * to * for 14 sts, navy (yb).

Rep group No. 1 until there are 12 ridges of garter st in orange (block No. 2).

Group No. 2 (first side).

Block No. 1 (orange garter st face)—orange (yf), navy (yb). E: * k 1 navy, p 1 orange *, rep from * to * 18 sts.

Block No. 2 (navy st face)—F: * p 1 orange (yb), navy (yb) k 1, (yf), * rep from * to * 14 sts.

Group No. 2 (second side).

Block No. 1 (navy garter st face)—G: * K 1 orange (yb), p 1 navy (yf) * rep from * to * 18 sts, orange (yf).

Block No. 2 (orange st face)—H: * p 1 navy (yb), k 1 orange (yf) * rep from * to * 14 sts. End with orange (yb), navy (yf).

Rep Group No. 2 until there are 8 ridges on each side in orange.

To begin, cast on with two colors using the two end of yarn method.

1st square—* start with orange (1st st), navy (2nd st), pull two orange ends between two navy ends and cast on orange, pull navy between two orange ends and cast on navy, * rep * to * for 18 sts ending in navy, put on marker.

2nd square—* cast on navy, pull navy between orange and cast on with orange, pull navy between orange and cast on. Continue in this manner for 14 sts, ending with orange.*

Repeat the above two blocks 5 times, repeat first block. This will give 178 sts on needle.

Follow directions for groups 1 and 2, repeat 7 times. Repeat Group No. 1, cast off with navy.

Cast off in this manner: K 2 tog, k 2 tog, pso, continue in this manner until the end. Cut yarn and pull end through loop. Use this same method with either one or more colors. With this rug, cast off with navy. At each

end of rug, work one row of sc with navy. Start and end with navy. No blocking is necessary.

Fringe—For each unit of fringe, use 4 ends of 1 color 20 inches long. At each corner pull the 4 ends of orange through, use an overhand knot to tie the 8 ends together. At either side of orange, repeat with blue. Trim to desired length. If you prefer, you can use fringe instead.

Crochet Rug (right in photo)

Materials
Aunt Lydia's Rug Yarn, 70-yd. skeins

8 lt. blue (A)
8 rust (B)
4 parchment (C)
2 med. blue (D)
Size I aluminum crochet hook

Gauge
4 dc = 1 inch, 10 rows = 6 inches

Directions
Using one strand color A, ch 111.
Row 1: Work 2 dc in second ch from hook, 1 dc in each of next 3 ch, sk 2 ch, * 1 dc in each of next 4 ch, 3 dc in next ch, 1 dc in each of next 4 ch, sk 2 ch, rep from * to last 4 ch. Work 1 dc in each of next 3 ch, 2 dc in last ch. Ch 2, turn.

Row 2: Work 2 dc in 3rd loop from hook, 1 dc in each of next 3 dc, sk 2 dc, * 1 dc in each of next 4 dc, 3 dc in next dc, 1 dc in each of next 4 dc, sk 2 dc, rep from * across to last 4 dc. Work 1 dc in each of next 3 dc, 2 dc in last dc.

Rep row 2 for pattern. Work 2 more rows A, 2 rows B, 1 row C, 1 row D, 1 row C, 2 rows B. Rep these 11 rows for entire rug, ending with 4 more rows A.

Clip yarn ends to within one inch and weave into work.

Accessories

Little things can often mean a lot in home decorating. An interesting accent like a crocheted basket or a knitted pillow may be just the spice you need to give your home that certain something extra. Handcrafted accessories are also ideal gifts for such occasions as house-warmings, weddings, and even holiday giving for family and friends. You'll find lots of ways to use the crocheted and knitted accessories you make, and this section is full of great ideas to choose from. For example, if you'd enjoy a doily-type table mat, make one like the unusual star pictured here. Directions for this unique piece of crochet follow on pages 70 and 71. Or if your taste runs to the rugged, contemporary look, pick from our basket collection. Fabulous pillows and lovely casement-like crocheted curtains are still more of the exciting accessories you'll find here.

Star Doily or Table Mat *(shown on pages 68-69)*

The eight-pointed star-shaped doily pictured on the previous pages measures 20½ inches in diameter. For the crocheting enthusiast, this project offers a great opportunity to use small amounts of leftover crochet thread from former projects.

Make it up in a combination of your favorite colors, or in a solid color, such as white or ecru.

Materials
J&P Coats
Knit Cro-Sheen
  1 black
  1 rust
  1 lt. green
  1 blue
  1 dk. red
  1 tan
  1 orange
Size 10 steel crochet hook

Directions
At center with first color, ch 6. Join with sl to form ring. Rnd 1: Ch 3 (to count as one dc), 23 dc in ring. Join with sl st to top of ch-3.

Rnd 2: Ch 3, dc in same place as sl st, dc in next dc, 2 dc in next dc, ch 1, * 2 dc in next dc, dc in next dc, 2 dc in next dc, ch 1. Rpt from * around. Join last ch 1 to top of ch-3 — 8 groups.

Rnd 3: Ch 3, dc in same place as sl st, * dc in 3 dc, 2 dc in next dc, ch 2, 2 dc in next dc. Rpt from * around joining last ch 2 to top of ch-3.

Rnd 4: Ch 3, dc in same place, * dc in each dc to last dc of this group; 2 dc in last dc, ch 3, 2 dc in next dc. Rpt from * around. Join.

Rnds 5 and 6: Work as for rnd 3 having ch 4 bet groups on rnd 5; ch 5 bet groups on rnd 6 — 13 dc in each group. Fasten off at end of rnd 6. Attach 2nd color to last joining.

Rnds 7 and 8: Work as for rnd 3 having ch 6 bet groups on each rnd — 17 dc in each group. Fasten off. Attach 3rd color as before.

Rnd 9: Ch 3, dc in same place, * dc in 7 dc, ch 2, sk next dc, dc in next 7 dc, 2 dc in last dc, ch 6, 2 dc in next dc. Rpt from * around. Join.

Rnd 10: Ch 3, dc in next 7 dc, * ch 2, 3 dc in sp, ch 2, sk next dc, dc in 8 dc, ch 6, dc in next 8 dc. Rpt from * around. Join.

Rnd 11: Ch 3, dc in same place, * dc in next 6 dc (ch 2, 3 dc in sp) twice; ch 2, sk next dc, dc in 6 dc, 2 dc in next dc, ch 6, 2 dc in next dc. Rpt from * around. Join.

Rnd 12: Ch 3, dc in next 6 dc, * ch 2, 3 dc in sp, ch 8, thread over hook 6 times, insert hook in center sp and pull through — 8 lps on hook; (thread over and draw through 2 lps) 7 times — long st made; ch 8, 3 dc in next sp, ch 2, sk next dc, dc in 7 dc, ch 6, dc in next 7 dc. Rpt from * around. Join.

Rnd 13: Ch 3, dc in next 5 dc, * ch 2, 3 dc in sp, ch 8, sc in top of ch 1p, sc in long st, sc in top of ch 1p, ch 8, 3 dc in next sp, ch 2, sk next dc, dc in 6 dc, ch 6, dc in next 6 dc. Rpt from *. Join.

Rnd 14: Ch 3, dc in next 4 dc, * ch 2, 3 dc in sp, ch 8, sc in top of ch, sc in 3 sc, sc in top of ch, ch 8, 3 dc in sp, ch 2, sk next dc, dc in 5 dc, ch 6, dc in 5 dc. Rpt from * around. Join.

Rnd 15: Ch 3, dc in next 3 dc, * ch 2, 3 dc in sp, ch 8, sc in ch, sc in 5 sc, sc in ch, ch 8, 3 dc in next sp, ch 2, sk next dc, dc in 4 dc, ch 6, dc in 4 dc. Rpt from * around. Join; fasten off. Attach 4th color as before.

Rnd 16: Ch 3, dc in next 2 dc. *Ch 2, 3 dc in sp, ch 8, sc in 7 sc, ch 8, 3 dc in sp, ch 2, sk next dc, dc in 3 dc, ch 6, dc in 3 dc. Rpt from * around. Join.

Rnd 17: Ch 3, dc in next 2 dc, * 3 dc in sp, ch 2, 3 dc in ch lp, ch 8, sc in 7 sc, ch 8, 3 dc in ch lp, ch 2, 3 dc in sp, dc in 3 dc, ch 6, dc in 3 dc. Rpt from * around. Join.

Rnd 18: Ch 3, dc in next 5 dc, * 3 dc in sp, ch 2, 3 dc in ch lp, ch 8, sk next sc, sc in 5 sc, ch 8, 3 dc in ch lp, ch 2, 3 dc in sp, dc in 6 dc, ch 6, dc in 6 dc. Rpt from * around. Join.

Rnd 19: Ch 3, dc in next 8 dc, * 3 dc in sp, ch 2, 3 dc in ch lp, ch 8, sk next sc, sc in 3 sc, ch 8, 3 dc in ch lp, ch 2, 3 dc in sp, dc in 9 dc, ch 6, dc in 9 dc. Rpt from * around. Join; fasten off. Attach 5th color as before.

Rnd 20: Ch 3, dc in next 11 dc, * 3 dc in sp, ch 2, 3 dc in ch lp, ch 5, thread over hook 4 times; pull up a lp in center sc — 6 lps on hook; (thread over hook and draw through 2 lps) 5 times — a long st made; ch 5, 3 dc in ch lp, ch 2, 3 dc in sp, dc in 12 dc, ch 6, dc in 12 dc. Rpt from * around. Join.

Rnd 21: Ch 3, dc in 14 dc, * 3 dc in sp, ch 2, 3 dc in lp, ch 3, sk long st, 3 dc in lp, ch 2, 3 dc in sp, dc in 15 dc, ch 6, dc in 15 dc. Rpt from * around. Join.

Rnd 22: Ch 3, dc in same place as sl st, * dc in 17 dc, 3 dc in sp, (ch 2, 3 dc in next sp) twice; dc in 17 dc, 2 dc in next dc, ch 6, 2 dc in next dc. Rpt from * around. Join; fasten off. Attach 6th color as before.

First point — Row 1: Ch 3, sk first dc, draw up a lp in each of next 2 dc, (thread over and draw through 2 lps) twice — dec made; dc in 17 dc, (ch 2, 3 dc in sp) twice; ch 2, sk 2 dc, dc in 19 dc. Ch 3, turn.

Row 2: Sk first dc, make a dec, dc in 14 dc, ch 2, 3 dc in sp, ch 6, dtr in next sp, ch 6, 3 dc in sp, ch 2, sk 2 dc, dc in 16 dc. Ch 3, turn.

Row 3: Sk first dc, make a dec, dc in 11 dc, ch 2, 3 dc in sp, ch 6, sc in ch lp, sc in dtr, sc in ch lp, ch

Filet Crochet Chair Set

6, 3 dc in sp, ch 2, sk 2 dc, dc in 13 dc. Fasten off. Attach 3rd color to last dc made, ch 3 turn.

Row 4: Sk first dc, make a dec, dc in 8 dc, ch 2, 3 dc in sp, ch 6, sc in ch lp, sc in 3 sc, sc in ch lp, ch 6, 3 dc in sp, ch 2, sk 2 dc, dc in 10 dc. Ch 3, turn.

Row 5: Sk first dc, make a dec, dc in 5 dc, ch 2, 3 dc in sp, ch 6, sc in ch lp, sc in 5 sc, sc in ch lp, ch 6, 3 dc in sp, ch 2, sk 2 dc, dc in 7 dc. Ch 3, turn.

Row 6: Sk first dc, make a dec, dc in 2 dc, 3 dc in sp, ch 8, sc in 7 sc, ch 8, 3 dc in sp, sk 2 dc, dc in 4 dc. Ch 3, turn.

Row 7: Sk first dc, make a dec, dc in next dc, ch 3, 3 dc in ch lp, ch 8, sk next sc, sc in 5 sc, ch 8, 3 dc in ch lp, ch 3, sk 3 dc, dc in next 3 dc. Ch 4, turn.

Row 8: 3 dc in sp, ch 3, 3 dc in lp, ch 8, sk next sc, sc in 3 sc, ch 8, 3 dc in lp, ch 3, 3 dc in sp, tr in last dc. Ch 4, turn.

Row 9: 3 dc in sp, ch 3, 3 dc in lp, ch 8, sc in center sc, ch 8, 3 dc in lp, ch 3, 3 dc in sp, tr in last dc. Ch 4, turn.

Row 10: 3 dc in sp, ch 3, 3 dc in lp, ch 4, dtr in sc, ch 4, 3 dc in lp, ch 3, 3 dc in sp, tr in last dc. Ch 3, turn.

Row 11: 3 dc in space, (ch 3, 3 dc in lp) twice; ch 3, 3 dc in sp, tr in last dc. Ch 4, turn.

Row 12: 3 dc in sp, (ch 3, 3 dc in sp) twice; tr in last dc. Ch 4, turn.

Row 13: 3 dc in sp, dc in 3 dc, 3 dc in sp, tr in last dc. Fasten off. Attach 7th color to last tr made; ch 3, turn.

Row 14: Sk tr and dc, make a dec, dc in 4 dc, make a dec. Ch 3, turn.

Row 15: Sk dc, make a dec, dc in 3 dc. Ch 3, turn.

Row 16: Sk dc, makes 2 decs. Fasten off. *Sk next ch-6 on doily, attach 6th color to next dc. Rpl rows 1 through 16 of first point. Rpt from * around.

Border: Attach first color to a ch-6 bet points, ch 1, 2 sc in same chain, ** ch 6, * sk next row, in end of next row make dc, ch 3, sc in 3rd ch from hook—picot made and dc; ch 4, sk next row, sc in end of next row, ch 4. Rpt from * along entire edge of this point, ch 6, 2 sc in next ch-6 bet points. Rep from ** around. Join; fasten off.

To block, stretch and pin doily to a padded surface. Cover with a wet cloth so doily feels damp, and allow to dry before removing pins. Or gently steam press with a warm iron. Hand wash in mild soap and warm water.

CROCHET HOOK SIZES

You can refer to the chart below to convert conventional crochet hook sizes to their nearest equivalent metric size.

LETTER EQUIVALENT	MILLIMETERS (MM)
B	2.00
C	2.50
D	3.00
E	3.50
F	4.00
G	4.50
H	5.00
I	5.50
	6.00
J	6.50
K	7.00
	8.00
	9.00
P	10.00

In our grandmother's day, fancy chair sets like the one shown on the following page were used to protect the backs and arms of fine parlor furniture. And since nothing ordinary would have been considered appropriate, these antimacassars –as they were called– were often beautiful and imaginative pieces of needlework.

With today's return to nostalgia in home decor, antimacassars are right back in style. And this one is especially delightful.

Materials

J & P Coats "Big Ball" Best Six Cord Mercerized Cotton, Art 105, size 30 or
Clark's "Big Ball" Mercerized Cotton, Art. B. 34, size 30 or
Clark's "Big Ball" Mercerized Cotton, Art. B. 345, size 30
2 balls No. 1 white
Size 10 steel crochet hook

Gauge

5 blocks or spaces = 1 inch; 6 rows = 1 inch
Note: Be sure to check your gauge before starting item. Use any size hook that will obtain stitch gauge above.

Directions

Arm cover (make 2)—Starting at lower edge, ch 27.

Row 1 (right side): Dc in 4th ch from hook and in next 2 ch—starting block made; dc in next 3 ch—another block made; make 6 more blocks. Ch 11, turn.

Row 2: Make a starting block and 2 blocks, working last dc of

continued

Filet Crochet
Chair Set *(continued)*

last block in first dc—3 blocks increased at beg of row; dc in next 3 dc—block over block made, make 1 more block, ch 2, sk 2 dc, dc in next dc—sp over block made, make 2 blocks, 1 sp and 1 block, dc in next 2 dc and in top of turning ch—block over block at end of row made, thread over, insert hook in same place as last dc and draw up a loop— 3 loops on hook—thread over and draw through 1 loop—this makes a ch st and 3 loops remain on hook—(thread over and draw through 2 loops) twice—foundation dc made; thread over, insert hook in the ch st at base of previous foundation dc and draw up a loop, thread over and draw through 1 loop, (thread over and draw through 2 loops) twice—another foundation dc made; make another foundation dc to complete a block—1 block increased at end of row; inc 2 more blocks at end of row. Ch 11, turn.

Row 3: Inc 3 blocks at beg of row, make 2 more blocks, 1 sp, 2 blocks, 2 dc in ch 2 sp, dc in next dc—block over sp made, 5 blocks, 1 sp, 2 blocks, inc 3 blocks at end of row. Ch 11, turn.

Row 4: Inc 3 blocks at beg of row, make 2 blocks, 1 sp, 5 blocks, 1 sp, 2 blocks, 1 sp, 5 blocks, 1 sp, 2 blocks; inc 3 blocks at end of row. Ch 3, turn.

Row 5: Dc in next 3 dc—starting block over block made, make 1 block, 1 sp, 5 blocks, 1 sp, 3 blocks, 2 sps, (1 block, 1 sp) twice; 5 blocks, 1 sp, and 2 blocks. Ch 5, turn.

Row 6: Starting block at beg of row—1 block increased at beg of row; make 5 blocks, 1 sp, 2 blocks, (1 sp, 1 block) twice; 2 sps, 3 blocks, 1 sp, 2 blocks, 1 sp, 5 blocks, inc 1 block at end of row. Ch 8, turn.

Row 7: Starting block at beg of row, make 1 more block—2

blocks increased at beg of row; make (1 sp, 2 blocks) 3 times; 1 sp, 3 blocks, 2 sps, (1 block, 1 sp) twice; (2 blocks, 1 sp) 3 times, working the dc of last sp in top of ch 3; inc 2 blocks at end of row. Ch 5, turn.

Starting with row 8, follow chart, reading from right to left on all odd-numbered rows and from left to right on all even-numbered rows until 31 rows have been completed. Turn.

Row 32: Sl st in each of first 4 dc, ch 3—1 block decreased at beg of row; complete first block, make 1 block more, 1 sp, 2 blocks, 1 sp, 1 block, 7 sps, 3 blocks, 2 sps, 1 block, 1 sp, 1 block, 5 sps, 1 block, 1 sp, 2 blocks, 1 sp, 2 blocks, leave remaining 2 dc and turning ch

unworked—1 block decreased at end of row. Turn.

Starting with row 33, complete arm cover. Follow chart.

Chair back—Starting at lower edge, ch 54.

Row 1 (right side): Make starting block and 17 more blocks. Ch 17, turn.

Row 2: Make starting block and 4 more blocks—5 blocks increased at beg of row; complete row following chart. Read from right to left, including *center*, then for other half of row omit *center*, and follow chart back again to right edge, increasing 5 blocks at end of row. Starting with row 2, complete remainder of chair back. Follow chart in same way.

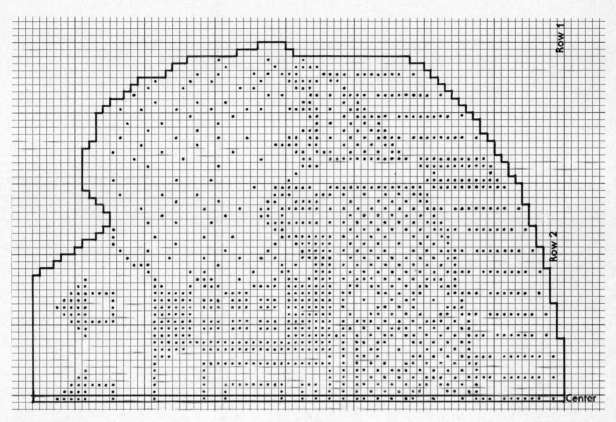

Row 1

Row 2

Center

⊡ = space

□ = block

Chair Back

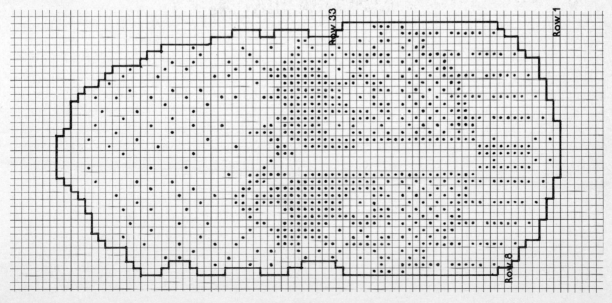

Row 33

Row 1

Row 8

Arm

Indian Design Baskets

This quartet of crocheted baskets, with shapes and motifs adapted from American Indian Designs, is truly an inspired project you'll want to make for gift-giving occasions or simply for your own enjoyment. The shallow basket tray at the far right shows figures with hands locked together celebrating the sun dance. Shells and beads adorn the necks of others. All are made from easy-to-find materials.

Beaded Oval Jute Basket

(No. 1 in drawing)

Materials

3 ply jute
  1 ball rust (R)
  1 ball natural (N)
  1 ball black (B)
Size H crochet hook
Heavy black thread
Darning needle
30 3/8-inch hishi beads (or 30 two-hole shirt buttons)
30 1/8-inch black beads with holes

Note: Do *not* join rnds. Place a safety pin in last st of every rnd to ensure proper shaping and counting. Move pin at end of each rnd.

To introduce new colors: Lay new color yarn along back of work and crochet over for about 5 sts.

To pick up new colors or change colors: When working last st of old color, insert hook into last st, draw loop through, drop old color, yo and draw loop through new color.

To dec 1 over 2 sts: *
Insert hook in first st, draw up loop, insert hook in next st, draw up loop * , yo and draw yarn through 3 loops on hook.

To change color after a dec: Rep from * to * (above), drop old color, yo and draw loop through new color.

Reverse sc: Ch 1, * insert hook in st to right of ch, draw loop through with a downward twist so that to yo, the yarn must come over the edge to create a beaded effect. *

Directions

Starting at the center of bottom with R, ch 8.

Rnd 1: 4 sc in second ch from hook, sc in next 5 ch, 4 sc in last ch; working along opposite side of starting ch, make sc in 5 ch—18 sc.

Rnd 2: (2 sc in each of next 4 sc, sc in next 5 sc) 2 times—26 sc. Rnd 3: * (Sc in next sc, 2 sc in next sc) 4 times; sc in next 5 sc. Rep from * once—34 sc. Rnd 4: Increasing 4 sc evenly spaced across each curved end, work sc in each sc—42 sc. Rnd 5: Sc in *back* lp of each sc around—42 sc. Attach B and N to wrong side of work.

Rnd 6: Hold unused colors along top of last rnd and work over them as follows: * Working in both lps with B, sc in next sc; pull up lp in next sc, drop B, pick up R and draw through 2 lps on hook (Color changed in last sc of a color group; always change color in this way). With R, make 2 sc in next sc changing to B in last sc; with B sc in next 2 sc changing to N in last sc; with N, sc in next 2 sc changing to B in last sc. Rep from * around—48 sc—6 pat reps. Hereafter, change colors as directed in rnd 6.

Rnd 7: (1B sc, 2R sc, 1N sc, 2R sc, 1B sc, work 2B sc in next sc) 6 times—54 sc. Rnd 8: (2R, 4N, 2R, work 2B sc in next sc) 6 times—60 sc. Rnd 9: (1R, 2N, 3B, 2N, 2R) 6 times; 1R in next sc,

move pin to last sc made—60 sc. Rnd 10: (2R, 4N, 2R, with B pull up lp in each of next 2 sc, drop B, with R yarn over hook and draw through all 3 lps on hook—a dec made and color changed) 6 times; 1B in next sc, move pin to last sc made—54 sc.

Rnd 11: (1B, 2R, 1N, 2R, 1B, with B dec over next 2 sc) 6 times—48 sc. Rnd 12: (1N, 2B, with R dec over next 2 sc, 2B, 1N) 6 times—42 sc. End off B and N. Rnd 13: With R (sc in 5 sc, dec over next 2 sc) 6 times—36 sc. Rnd 14: With R (sc in 4 sc, dec) 6 times—30 sc. S1 st in next sc. Rnd 15: Ch 1, working from left to right, work sc in each sc around. S1 st in next sc. End off.

Finishing—Sew one hishi bead to each sc on rnd 14 of the oval jute basket. Use heavy-duty black thread and a darning needle, and use the small black beads in the centers of the hishi beads.

Oval Basket (No. 2 in drawing)

Materials

Aunt Lydia's Rug Yarn, 70-yard skeins
  1 black (B)
  1 natural (N)
  1 antique gold (G)
Sizes F and G crochet hooks

Directions

Starting at center of bottom with *continued*

Indian Design Baskets *(continued)*

B and using a size F crochet hook, ch 4, Join with sl st to form ring. Rnd 1: Ch 1, 8 sc in ring.

Rnd 2: 2 sc in each sc around —16 sc. Rnd 3: (Sc in next sc, 2 sc in next sc) 8 times—24 sc.

Rnd 4: (Sc in 2 sc, 2 sc in next sc) 8 times—32 sc. Rnd 5: (Sc in 3 sc, 2 sc in next sc) 8 times—40 sc. Rnd 6: Sc in each sc—40 sc. Attach N and G to wrong side of work.

Rnd 7: Hold unused colors along top of last rnd and work over them as follows: * With B, pull up lp in next sc, drop B, pick up N and draw through 2 lps on hook (Color changed in last sc of a color group; always change color in this way). With N, sc in next 4 sc changing to G in last sc; with G, sc in next sc changing to N; with N, sc in next 4 sc changing to B in last sc. Rep from * 3 times more—40 sc—4 pat reps.

Rnd 8: * Insert hook through the front 2 vertical strands (not the top lps) of next B sc and pull B lp through, drop B and draw N through 2 lps on hook (a long B sc made and color changed); 4N sc in 4N sc changing to G in last sc, 2G in next G sc changing to N in last sc made; 4N sc in 4N sc changing to B in last sc. Rep from * 3 times more—44 sc.

Rnd 9: * Insert hook under the long B sc and pull B lp through, drop B and draw N through 2 lps on hook; 4N sc changing to G in last sc, 1G sc, 2G sc in next G sc changing to N; 4N sc changing to B in last sc. Rep from * around—48 sc. Rnd 10: * Working as for rnd 9, make 1 long B sc, 4N sc, 2G sc, 2G sc in next G sc, 4N sc. Rep from * around—52 sc.

Rnd 11: * Working as before, make 1 long B sc, 4N sc, 3G sc, 2G sc in next G sc, 4N sc. Rep from * around—56 sc. Rnd 12: Drop N to back of work. * 1 long B sc, 4B, 5G, 4B. Rep from * around— 56 sc. Rnd 13: * 1 long B sc, 4N,

5G, 4N. Rep from * around. Rnds 14, 15, and 16: Rep rnds 12, 13, and 12—56 sc.

Rnd 17: * 1 long B sc, 3N, with N pull up a lp in each of next 2 sc, drop N; with G yarn over hook and draw through all 3 lps on hook (a dec made and color changed); 4G, 4N. Rep from * around—52 sc. Rnd 18: Work as for rnd 17 having 1G sc less in each group—48 sc. Rnds 19 and 20: Rep rnd 18 2 times—40 sc— 1G sc left in each pat rep.

Rnd 21: * 1 long B sc, with N make a dec over next 2 sc, 2N, 1G, with N make a dec, 2N. Rep from * around—32 sc. Rnd 22: Work as for rnd 21 having 1N sc less in each N panel—24 sc—2N sc left in each N panel. Rnds 23 through 28: Work color over color—24 sc. Rnd 29: * 1 long B sc, 2B, 1G, 2B. Rep from * around. Rnd 30: * 1 long B sc, 2N, 1G, 2N. Rep from * around.

Rnds 31 through 35: Rep rnds 29 and 30 alternately twice; then rep rnd 29 once more. End off N and G. Rnd 36: Change to size H hook. With B, sl st in next sc, ch 1; working from *left to right*, work sc in each sc around. Sl st in next sc. End off.

Shell Basket *(No. 3 in drawing)*

Materials

Aunt Lydia's Rug Yarn, 70 yd. skeins
  1 copper (C)
  1 black (B)
  6 yds. parchment (P)
Size G aluminum crochet hook
12 to 15 cowrie shell beads
for basket neck

Directions

Starting at center of bottom with C, ch 4. Join with sl st to form ring. Rnd 1: Ch 1, 7 sc in ring. Rnd 2: 2 sc in each sc around— 14 sc. Rnd 3: (Sc in next sc, 2 sc in next sc) 7 times—21 sc.

Rnds 4 through 7: Increasing 7

sc, evenly spaced on each rnd, work sc in each sc—49 sc—at end of rnd 7. Rnd 8: Sc in each sc increasing one sc—50 sc. Attach B to wrong side of work. Hold unused color along top of last rnd and work over it as follows: With C, pull up a lp in next sc, drop C, pick up B and draw through 2 lps on hook. Move pin to last sc made to mark end of rnd. Working over unused color, continue as follows:

Rnd 9: * With B, pull up lp in next sc, drop B, pick up C and draw through 2 lps on hook (Color changed in last sc of a color group; always change color in this way). With C, sc in next 9 sc changing to B in last sc. Rep from * 4 times more—50 sc —5 pat reps.

Rnd 10: * With B, 2 sc in next sc changing to C in last sc; with C pull up a lp in each of next 2 sc, yarn over hook and draw through all 3 lps on hook (dec made); sc in next 7 sc changing to B in last sc. Rep from * around —50 sc.

Rnd 11: * With B, sc in next sc, 2 sc in next sc changing to C in last sc; with C make a dec over next 2 sc, sc in next 6 sc changing to B in last sc. Rep from * around—50 sc. Rnd 12: * 2B sc, 2B sc in next sc changing to C; with C dec over next 2 sc, sc in 5 sc changing to B. Rep from * around—50 sc. Attach P to back of work.

Rnd 13: * Make 2B sc changing to P; with P sc in same place where last sc was made, changing to B; 2B changing to C; with C make a dec and 3 sc changing to B. Rep from * around—50 sc. Rnd 14: * 2B, 2P sc in next sc, 2B, with C make a dec and 2 sc changing to B. Rep from * around—50 sc. Rnd 15: * 2B, 2P, 2B, (with C, dec over next 2 sc) 1 time changing to B. Rep from * around—40 sc.

Rnd 16: * 2B, with P make a

dec, 2B, with C make a dec changing to B. Rep from * around—30 sc. End off P and C. Rnd 17: With B sc in each sc around. Rnds 18 and 19: Decreasing 5 sc evenly spaced on each rnd, sc in each sc—20 sc. Rnd 20: Sc in 20 sc, sl st in next sc. Rnd 21: Ch 1, working from *left to right*, work sc in each sc around. Sl st in next sc. End off.

Finishing—With thread and darning needle, sew cowrie shell beads around top between rnds 18 and 19.

Shallow Figured Basket
(No. 4) in drawing)

Materials
Coats and Clark's Speed-Cro-Sheen
1 tangerine (T)
1 nu ecru (E)
1 fudge brown (B)
Size 2 steel crochet hook

Directions
Cut off a 1-yard strand of T. Starting at center with T, ch 4. Join with sl st to form ring.

Rnd 1: Ch 1, working over the 1-yard strand, make 8 sc in ring.

Rnd 2: Working over the strand, 2 sc in each sc—16 sc. Continue working over the strand.

Rnd 3: (Sc in next sc, 2 sc in next sc) 8 times—24 sc. Rnds 4 and 5: Increasing 8 sc, evenly spaced on each rnd, sc in each sc—40 sc at end of rnd 5. Sl st in next sc. End off T, remove pin. Attach B in any sc on last rnd. Rnd 6: Ch 1, sc where B was attached, sc in next 3 sc, 2 sc in next sc, (sc in 4 sc, 2 sc in next sc) 7 times—48 sc. Attach E to wrong side of work; with B pull up a lp in next sc, drop B, pick up E and draw through 2 lps on hook (color changed). Place pin in last sc made to mark end of rnd. Hold unused color along top

of last rnd and work over it as follows:

Rnd 7: * With E, sc in next sc, pull up a lp in same sc, drop E, pick up B and draw through 2 lps on hook (Color changed in last sc of a color group; always change color in this way). With B, sc in next 2 sc changing to E in last sc; with E, sc in next sc changing to B; with B, sc in next 2 sc changing to E. Rep from * around—56 sc—8 pat reps.

Rnd 8: * With E, sc in 4 sc changing to B in last sc; with B, sc in same sc where last sc was made changing to E; with E, sc in next sc changing to B; with B, sc in next sc changing to E; with E, sc in next sc. Rep from * around—64 sc. Hereafter, change colors as directed.

Rnd 9: * 5E, 1B in same place where last sc was made; 1E, 1B, 1E. Rep from * around—72 sc. Rnd 10: (3E, 1B in same sc; 8B, 4E, 1B in same sc; 2B, 1E) 4 times—80 sc. Rnd 11: (5E, 1B in same sc; 6B, 6E, 1B in same sc; 2B, 1E) 4 times—88 sc.

Rnd 12: (7E, 1B in same sc; 4B, 8E, 1B in same sc; 2B, 1E) 4 times—96 sc. Rnd 13: (3E, 2B, 4E, 1B in same sc; 2B, 1E) 8 times—104 sc. Rnd 14: * (1E, 3B) 2 times; 2E, 1B in same sc; 2B, 1E. Rep from * around ending last rep with 3B (instead of 2B, 1E)—112 sc.

Rnd 15: * 2B, 2E, with E pull up a lp in each of next 2 sc, yarn over hook and draw through all 3 lps on hook; 2E, 1B in same sc, 8B, 6E, 1B in same sc; 6B. Rep from * around ending last rep with 5 (instead of 6) B—116 sc. Rnd 16: 13E, 1B in same sc; (15E, 1B in same sc; 14E, 1B in same sc) 3 times; 15E, 1B in same sc—124 sc. Move pin to last sc made.

Rnd 17: (14E, 1B in same sc; 2B) 2 times; (13E, 1B in same sc; 2B, 14E, 1B in same sc; 2B) 3 times—132 sc. Move pin to last

sc. Rnd 18: (14E, 1B in same sc; 2B, 15E, 1B in same sc; 2B) 4 times—140 sc. Rnd 19: (Working over B as before, with E sc in 6 sc, 2 sc in next sc, sc in 28 sc) 4 times—144 sc. End off B, attach T to wrong side.

Rnd 20: Working over E, (3T, inc in next sc; 12T, 2E) 8 times—152 sc. Rnd 21: 16T, 5E, (7T, inc in next sc; 6T, 5E, 14T, 5E) 3 times; 7T, inc; 6T, 5E—156 sc. Move pin to last sc. Rnd 22: 6T, inc; 6T, 8E, (12T, 8E, 5T, inc; 5T, 8E) 3 times; 12T, 8E—160 sc. Move pin.

Rnd 23: 14T, 5E, (5T, inc; 9T, 5E, 15T, 5E) 3 times; 1T—164 sc. Rnd 24: 9T, inc; 6T, 2E, (19T, 2E, 11T, inc; 6T, 2E) 3 times; 19T, 2E, 2T—168 sc. Rnd 25: Working over E, sc in each sc around. End off E, attach B. Rnd 26: Working over T, sc in each sc around. End off T. With B, sl st in *back* lp of each sc around; sl st in first sl st. End off.

Finishing—Basket may be stiffened with spray starch. Spray, flatten, and shape basket with your fingers; allow to dry.

CROCHETED BASKETS

When it comes to crocheting baskets, the only limitations are your own imagination and ingenuity.

■ *Use a variety of materials. Jute, rug yarn, straw-like yarn, and different weights of packaging cord are all good choices.*
■ *If you're groping for design ideas, explore museums, art fairs, and antique shows as well as gift shops and basketry departments in larger stores.*
■ *Decide what size and shape baskets are best for your needs. If you want to nestle plant containers in them, measure your pots and allow a little extra space for sliding them in and out.*

Crocheted Cord Baskets

Common, everyday cotton cord takes on an exciting new dimension when you use it to crochet novelty baskets, such as the two pictured on the opposite page. In addition to adding decorative accents, they also provide storage for many items.

These crocheted baskets are inexpensive and easy to make, and work up amazingly fast.

Round Basket (left in photo)

Materials
3 ply cotton cord
   75 yds. (approximately)
Size K crochet hook

Finished size
Approximately 9 inches in diameter and 6 inches high

Directions
Bottom of basket—Ch 5: join with sl st to form ring. Ch 1 to begin second rnd.

Rnd 1: Inc by working 2 sc in every st of base ch.

Rnd 2: Repeat rnd 1.

Rnd 3: Continue to sc, increasing with 2 sc in every other sc of preceding rnd.

Rnd 4: Inc with 2 sc in every fourth sc of preceding rnd.

Rnd 5: Inc with 2 sc in every sixth sc of preceding rnd.

Rnd 6: Inc with 2 sc in every eighth sc of preceding rnd.

Sides of basket—Rnd 1: Ch 3 (counting as first dc), then dc around base in every st. Join last dc to first dc with a sl st, then ch 3 for beginning of second rnd.

Rnd 2 and 3: Continue to dc in every stitch in preceding rnds.

Rnd 4: Inc by crocheting 2 dc in every eighth st of preceding rnd (this is the last inc rnd).

Rnd 5: This will be the first row of scalloped edging. There are 3 ch sts per scallop. After attaching last dc of preceding rnd with a sl st, ch 3; sk two sts of preceding rnd and attach chain to third st of preceding rnd with a sc. Work 3 more ch sts, sk 2 sts of preceding rnd, and attach ch to third st with a sc. Repeat scallop pattern around entire rim of basket.

Rnd 6: Repeat rnd 5, joining each ch scallop from center top of one scallop on preceding rnd to center top of adjacent scallop.

Rnd 7: Repeat rnd 6, end off cord, and weave in loose ends with crochet hook.

Oval Basket (right in photo)

Materials
3 ply cotton cord
   65 yds. (approximately)
Size K crochet hook

Finished Size
Approximately 5½ inches high, 9 inches wide, and 5½ inches deep

Directions
Bottom of basket—Ch 12.

Rnd 1: Ch 2 for beginning of rnd, then sc to end of base ch. Ch 2 (to ease around curve at end of base ch), then sc down other side of base ch. Mark end of ch so you can count rnds.

Rnds 2, 3, 4: Continue to sc up and down base ch, increasing with a ch st after every two sc sts at end of base ch (to ease curve). In all, there should be four rows of sc on either side of base ch.

Sides of basket—Rnd 1: Ch 3 for beginning of dc row. Dc around base in every stitch. Join last dc of this rnd to first dc with a ch st. Ch 3 for beginning of second rnd.

Rnd 2: Repeat dc pattern, but inc around curves at ends of the oval by crocheting two dc in every third st around the curve. No increase around sides.

Rnd 3: Every sixth st, dc two sts in one dc of preceding rnd. This will give a slightly flared shape to basket.

Rnd 4: This will be the first row of ch scallops. To make scallop edging, follow instructions for rnds 5-7 of sides of round basket given above. End off cord, and weave in loose ends with crochet hook.

CROCHET HOOKS

Although crochet hooks are available in a variety of materials and a broad range of sizes, they are all basically the same shape. The thickness of the shaft, or shank, determines the size of each stitch and the hook at the end catches the yarn.

■ *The most widely used hooks are made of aluminum because it is lightweight, strong, and smooth. Also, they come in many sizes.*

■ *Plastic hooks, except for the very large sizes which you would use only for very thick yarns, cords, or rope, are not advised. In the smaller sizes, they become brittle and break easily.*

■ *Steel hooks come in the smaller sizes, usually have a sharper point, and are used for lace-type crocheting that requires fine crochet threads.*

■ *You will also find some wooden hooks, but these are not as durable as the aluminum and steel hooks, except in the very large sizes.*

■ *The hook size given with instructions is based on average tension. If you crochet tighter or looser than the average, use a larger or smaller hook to achieve the correct gauge.*

Crocheted Butterfly Pillow and Knitted Patchwork Pillow

Be as daring as you please when you choose the colors for either of these smashing pillow designs. The knitted patchwork pillow is an easily achieved design you can whip up from leftover bits of yarn. The butterfly pillow is also lovely in pastels.

Butterfly Pillow

Materials

Knitting worsted-weight yarn, 2 oz. skeins
 1 turquoise
 1 green
 1 purple
 1 pink
 1 yellow
 1 black
Size H crochet hook
15x36-inch piece of velveteen
Batting for stuffing

Directions

Right wing (top section)—With turquoise, ch 22.

Rnd 1: 2 sc in 2nd ch from hook, sc in next 6 ch, hdc in next 3 ch, dc in next 10 ch, 8 dc in last ch; then working along opposite side of starting ch, make dc in 10 ch, hdc in 3 ch, sc in 7 ch. Join with sl st to first sc.

Rnd 2: Ch 1, sc in same place as sl st, 3 sc in next sc, sc in next 6 sc, hdc in 3 hdc, dc in 11 dc, 2 dc in each of next 7 dc, dc in 10 dc, hdc in 3 hdc, sc in 6 sc, 3 sc in last sc. Join.

Rnd 3: Ch 1, sc in same place as sl st, sc in next sc, 3 sc in next sc; then increasing 6 sc evenly spaced across curved end, work sc in each st and 3 sc in last sc. Join and fasten off.

Wing tip—Mark off the center 18 sc on curved end. With right side facing, attach yellow to first

marked sc, ch 1, sc in next 4 sc, (2 sc in next sc, sc in next 2 sc) 4 times; sl st in next sc. Fasten off.

Center section—With green, work same as top section until rnd 3 has been completed. (Use photo as a guide.) Then, catching both loops of scs on each section and starting at center sc of a 3 sc group at narrow end, overcast edges tog to first yellow sc on top section.

Bottom section—With purple, ch 17. Rnd 1: 2 sc in second ch from hook, sc in next 4 ch, hdc in 3 ch, dc in 7 ch, 8 dc in last ch; working along opposite side of starting chain, make dc in 7 ch, hdc in 3 ch, sc in 5 ch. Join.

Rnd 2: Ch 1, sc in same place as sl st, 3 sc in next sc, sc in next 4 sc, hdc in next 3 hdc, dc in 8 dc, 2 dc in next 7 dc, dc in next 7 dc, hdc in next 3 hdc, sc in 4 sc, 3 sc in last sc. Join.

Rnd 3: Same as rnd 3 of top section.

Tip—Same as wing tip on top section. Working as before, overcast edge of bottom section to

center section from center sc of a 3 sc group to within 5 sc of first yellow sc on bottom section.

Left wing—Make sections same as right wing, but when sewing them tog, be sure to have both left and right wings. Overlap narrow edges for ½ inch and sew wings tog.

Border—With right side facing, attach pink to lower end of center seam. Rnd 1: Increasing 4 sc evenly spaced across curved end of each section, work sc in each sc around. Join.

Rnd 2: Ch 3, dc in each sc to within the seam that joins the bottom and center sections; insert hook through seam 1 inch in from edge and pull loop through, yo and complete a sc—long sc made; sk the sc under the long sc, dc in each sc to within 3 sc before the sc at the seam that joins the center and top sections, (yo, pull up a loop in next sc, yo and draw through 2 loops) twice; yo and draw through remaining 3 loops—one dc dec; (yo, pull up a loop in next sc, yo and draw through 2 loops) 3 times; yo and draw through remaining 4 loops—2 dc dec; dec 1 dc over next 2 sc, dc in each sc to center seam. Work remaining wing to correspond. Fasten off. Flatten piece out and pin to a padded surface; cover with a wet Turkish towel and allow to dry thoroughly.

Body—With yellow, ch 4. Join with sl st to form ring.

Rnd 1: Ch 1, 7 sc in ring. Do not join rnds.

Rnd 2: 2 sc in 7 sc.

Rnds 3, 4, 5: Sc in 14 sc.

Rnd 6: * Sc in 2 sc, pull up a loop in each of next 2 sc, yo and draw through 3 loops on hook—dec made. Rep from * until 8 sc remain. Stuff with batting. Work 3 rnds even. Adding stuffing as work progresses, * sc in 3 sc, 2 sc in next sc. Rep from * until there are 18 sc on rnd. Work 18 rnds even; then * sc in 10 sc, make a dec. Rep from * until 5 sc remain. Break off yarn, leaving a 6-inch end. Thread a needle with this end and draw remaining sts tog. With black, make French knots for eyes; make two 3-inch chains for antennae and sew in place.

Finishing—To make the pillow form, use the crocheted wings for a pattern, allowing ¾ inch all around for seam allowance. Use this pattern to cut out two pieces of velveteen. With the right sides together, sew the velveteen pillow pieces together ½ inch from the edge, leaving an opening for turning. Turn pillow right side out. Stuff lightly with batting; whipstitch opening closed. Mount the crocheted wings on the pillow form. Sew the body in place between the wings.

Patchwork Pillow

Materials

Knitting worsted-weight yarn,
2 oz. skeins
1 red
1 gold
1 yellow
1 black
2 blue
Size 8 knitting needles
Size H crochet hook
16x16-inch knife-edged pillow form

Directions

Top—First strip: With red, cast on 23 sts. Row 1: k 1, (p 3, k 6) twice; p 3, K 1.

Row 2: K 4, (p 6, k 3) twice; k 1.

Rows 3 through 6: Rep rows 1 and 2 alternately twice.

Row 7: K 1, (p 3, sl next 3 sts onto a toothpick and hold in front of work, k next 3 sts, k 3 sts from toothpick) twice; p 3, k 1.

Row 8: Rep row 2.

Rows 9 through 16: Rep rows 1 and 2 alternately 4 times.

Rows 17 and 18: Rep rows 7 and 2.

Rows 19 through 24: Rep rows 1 and 2 alternately 3 times. Break off red, attach yellow. Work 12 rows of garter st (k every row). Break off yellow, attach red. Work 17 rows of st st (k 1 row, p 1 row) ending with a k row. Break off red, attach gold and p 1 row.

Work in pat as follows. Row 1: K 1, p 4, (with yarn in back, sl 1, p 5) twice; sl 1, p 4, k 1.

Row 2: (K 5, p the slipped st) 3 times; k 5.

Row 3: Rep row 1.

Row 4: K across.

Rep rows 1 through 4 three times; then rep rows 1, 2, and 3. Break off gold, attach black. Starting with a p row, work 11 rows of st st. Bind off.

Pin out to measure 5x15 inches. Cover with a wet Turkish towel and allow to dry thoroughly. With blue, work 1 row of sc evenly along each long edge.

Second strip—With red, cast on 20 sts. Work 14 rows of garter st. Break off red, attach black. Row 1: K.

Row 2: P.

Rows 3 and 4: K.

Rep rows 1 through 4 six times. Break off black, attach gold and k across. Work in pat as follows.

Row 1 (wrong side): (k 4, p 1) 3 times; k 5.

Row 2: (K 1, p 4) 3 times; k 1, p 3, k 1. Rep rows 1 and 2 alternately 13 times. Break off gold, attach yellow and k across. Work in pat as follows. Row 1: K 2, (p 1, k 3) 4 times; p 1, k 1.

Row 2: (K 3, p 1) 4 times; k 4. Rep rows 1 and 2 alternately 7 times. Bind off.

Block to measure 4x15 inches and finish same as first strip.

Center strip—With gold, cast on 29 sts. Row 1: K 1, * p 1, k 1. Rep from * across. Rep row 1 11 times. Break off gold, attach yellow. Work 18 rows of st st. Break off yellow, attach black. Work 19 rows of garter st. Break off black, attach red and p 1 row, increasing 1 st—30 sts.

Work in pat as follows. Rows 1 through 4: (K 5, p 5) 3 times.

Rows 5 through 8: (P 5, k 5) 3 times. Rep rows 1 through 8 twice. Bind off.

Block to measure 6x15 inches and finish same as first strip.

Finishing—With blue, work 1 row sc along remaining two edges.

Back—With blue, make a ch 1 inch longer than one edge of top.

Row 1: Sc in second ch from hook, sc in each ch across. Ch 1, turn.

Row 2: Sc in each sc across. Ch 1, turn. Rep last row until piece is same size as top. Sew top and back tog along 3 edges. Insert pillow form and sew rem edge tog.

Granny Square Pillows

You'll discover it takes only slight variations on the all-time favorite granny squares to make the pair of eye-catching 18-inch-square reversible crocheted pillows that are pictured on the opposite page.

Blue-Green Reversible Pillow

Materials

Coats & Clark's Red Heart Knitting Worsted, 4 oz. skeins
1 blue
1 black
1 turquoise
2 lime
Size H crochet hook
18-inch knife-edged pillow form

Gauge

2 dc and ch 1 = ¾ inch; 2 dc and ch 1 = 1¼ inches

Directions

Motif (make 4)—Starting at center with black, ch 4. Join with sl st to form ring. Rnd 1: Ch 3 (to count as one dc), 11 dc in ring. Join with sl st to top of ch 3. Fasten off. Rnd 2: Attach blue between any two dc, ch 3, 2 dc in same place where yarn was attached, * 3 dc between next 2 dc. Rep from * around—36 dc. Join, fasten off.

Rnd 3: Attach lime between any 2 dc, ch 1, sc in same place, * ch 3, sk 3 dc, sc between last and next dc. Rep from * around joining last ch 3 to first sc—12 loops. Fasten off. Rnd 4: Attach black to any loop, ch 3, holding back on hook the last loop of each dc, make 2 dc in same loop, yo hook and draw through all 3 loops on hook, ch 2, holding back on hook the last loop of each dc, make 3 dc in same loop,

yarn over and draw through all 4 loops on hook—cluster made; * (ch 2, cluster in next loop) twice; ch 2, in next loop make cluster, ch 2 and cluster—corner made. Rep from * around joining last ch 2 to top of cluster—4 corners. Fasten off.

Rnd 5: Attach turquoise to any corner sp, ch 1, in same sp make 2 sc, ch 2 and 2 sc; * (ch 2, insert hook between last dc of next cluster and the lime sc below and draw loop through to height of last sc made, yo hook and draw through 2 loops on hook— long sc made) 3 times; ch 2, in corner sp make 2 sc, ch 2 and 2 sc. Rep from * around joining last ch 2 to first sc. Fasten off. Hereafter, attach designated color in any corner sp.

Rnd 6: Lime, ch 3, (in same sp make dc, ch 2 and 2 dc; * ch 1, (in next sp make dc, ch 1 and dc) 4 times; ch 1, in corner sp make 2 dc, ch 2 and 2 dc. Rep from * around. Join, fasten off. Rnd 7: Blue, ch 1, in same sp make sc, ch 2 and sc, * ch 1, sk 2 dc, 2 sc in next sp, (ch 1, 2 sc in next sp) 5 times; ch 1, in corner sp make sc, ch 2 and sc. Rep from * around. Join, fasten off. Motif measures about 6 inches square. With blue, sew 2x2 motifs tog, stitch for stitch and matching corners—about 12 inches square.

Border—Rnd 1: Turquoise, ch 1, sc, ch 2 and sc in same sp, (ch 2, sc in next sp) 7 times; ch 2 draw up a loop in each of the next 2 corner sps, yo and draw through all 3 loops on hook, (ch 2, sc in next sp) 7 times; ch 2, in corner sp make sc, ch 2 and sc. Rep from * around. Join 16 sps on each edge between corners. Do not fasten off.

Rnd 2: In corner sp make sl st, ch 3, 2 dc, ch 2 and 3 dc; * (3 dc in next sp) 16 times; in corner sp make 3 dc, ch 2 and 3 dc. Rep from * around. Join, fasten off. Rnd 3: Blue, ch 1, sc, ch 2 and sc

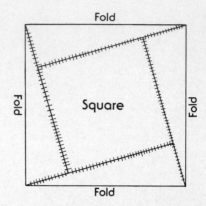

in same sp—starting sc corner made; * (ch 1, sk 3 dc, 2 sc between last and next dc) 17 times; ch 1, in corner sp make sc, ch 2 and sc—sc corner made. Rep from * around. Join, fasten off. Rnd 4: Lime, ch 1, starting sc corner in same sp, * (ch 1, 2 sc in next sp) 18 times; ch 1, sc corner in corner sp. Rep from * around. Join, do not fasten off until directed. Rnd 5: In corner sp make sl st, ch 3, dc, ch 2 and 2 dc—starting dc corner made; * ch 1, (2 dc in next sp, ch 1) 19 times; in corner sp make 2 dc, ch 2 and 2 dc—dc corner made. Rep from * around. Join.

Rnd 6: Sl st in next dc; then work as for rnd 5. Fasten off. Rnd 7: Black, work as for rnd 4. Fasten off. Rnds 8, 9 and 10: Turquoise, work as for rnds 4, 5, and 6. Rnd 11: Black, work as for rnd 4. Fasten off. Rnds 12, 13, and 14: Lime, work as for rnds 4, 5, and 6. Rnd 15: Black, work as for rnd 4. Fasten off.

Square—Work same as motif until rnd 5 has been completed. Rnd 6: Lime, starting dc corner in corner sp, ch 1, * (2 dc in next sp, ch 1) 4 times; dc corner in corner sp. Rep from * around. Join, fasten off. Rnd 7: Black, work as for rnd 4 of border. Fasten off. Rnd 8: Turquoise, *continued*

Granny Square Pillows *(continued)*

work as for rnd 6 of square. Do not fasten off. Rnd 9: Work as for rnd 6 of border.

Rnd 10: Blue, work as for rnd 4 of border. Fasten off. Rnds 11 through 14: Work as for rnds 12 through 15 of border.

Finishing—Place large piece, wrong side up, on a flat surface. Place square, wrong side down, at an angle, on top of and in center of large piece. Following diagram, fold edges of large piece over to edges of square, corners matching. Following dotted lines on diagram, sew 3 seams, stitch for stitch. Slip pillow form inside; sew last seam.

Red-Black Reversible Pillow

Materials
Coats & Clark's Red Heart Knitting Worsted, 4 oz. skeins
    2 black
    1 pink
    1 dk. red
    1 lt. red
    1 orange
    1 brown
Size H crochet hook
18-inch knife-edged pillow form

Gauge
2 3-dc groups = 1¾ inches; 2 dc rnds = 1¼ inches

Directions
Starting at center with light red, ch 4. Join with sl st to form ring. Rnd 1: Ch 4, (dc, ch 1) 11 times. Join with sl st to 3rd ch of ch 4—12 sps. Fasten off. Rnd 2: Attach brown in any sp, ch 3 (to count as one dc) 2 dc in same sp, 3 dc in each sp around. Join to ch 3—36 dc. Fasten off. Rnd 3: Attach black between any two dc, ch 1, sc in same place where yarn was attached, (ch 3, sk 3 dc, sc between last and next dc) 11 times; ch 1. Join to first sc—12 sps. Fasten off.

Rnd 4: Attach pink in any sp, ch 1, 3 sc in same sp, (ch 1, 3 sc in next sp) 11 times; ch 1—12 sps. Join, fasten off. Rnd 5: Attach light red in any sp, ch 3, 3 dc in same sp, 4 dc in each sp around—48 dc. Join, fasten off. Rnd 6: Attach black to first dc of any 4 dc group, ch 1, sc where yarn was attached, sc in next 3 dc, * insert hook in center sc of pink 3 sc group below and draw loop through to height of sc just made; yarn over and draw through 2 loops on hook—long sc made; long sc in same place as last long sc, sc in next 4 dc. Rep from * around ending with 2 long sc. Join, fasten off.

Rnd 7: Attach orange to the sc following a long sc, ch 1, sc in same place, * ch 3, sk 2 sts, sc in next st. Rep from * around joining last ch 3 to first sc—24 sps. Fasten off. Rnd 8: Attach pink in any sp, ch 3, in same sp make 2 dc, ch 2 and 3 dc—starting dc corner made; * (3 dc in next sp) 5 times; in next sp make 3 dc, ch 2 and 3 dc—dc corner made. Rep from * around—4 corners. Join, fasten off.

Rnd 9: Attach orange in sp of any corner, make a starting dc corner in same sp, * (sk 3 dc, 3 dc between last and next dc) 6 times; dc corner in sp of next corner. Rep from * around—4 corners. Join, fasten off. Hereafter, attach designated color in any corner sp.

Rnd 10: Dark red, ch 1, in same sp make sc, ch 2 and sc—starting sc corner made; * (ch 1, 2 long sc in center dc of next pink 3 dc group below) 7 times; ch 1, in corner sp make sc, ch 2 and sc—sc corner made. Rep from * around. Join, fasten off.

Rnd 11: Black, starting sc corner in same sp; * (ch 1, 2 sc in next sp) 8 times; ch 1, sc corner in corner. Rep from * around. Join, fasten off. Rnd 12: Dark red, starting dc corner in same

sp, * (ch 1, 2 dc in next sp) 9 times; ch 1, dc corner in corner. Rep from * around. Join, fasten off. Rnd 13: Black, starting dc corner in same sp, * 3 dc in each sp across to within next corner, dc corner in corner. Rep from * around. Join, fasten off.

Rnd 14: Orange, starting sc corner in same sp, * (ch 2, sk 3 dc, sc between last and next dc) 11 times; ch 2, sc corner in corner. Rep from * around. Join, fasten off. Rnd 15: Pink, rep rnd 13. Rnd 16: Orange, work as for rnd 9. Rnd 17: Light red, work as for rnd 10. Rnd 18: Dark red, work as for rnd 11. Rnd 19: Black, work as for rnd 12. Do *not* break off until directed. Rnd 20: Sl st in next 2 dc, sl st in corner sp, work as for rnd 13.

Rnd 21: Sl st in next 2 dc, sl st in corner sp, work as for rnd 9. Rnd 22: Rep rnd 21. Fasten off. Rnd 23: Brown, work as for rnd 10 making long scs in center dc of black group below. Join, fasten off. Rnd 24: Light red, work as for rnd 13. Rnd 25: Pink, starting dc corner in same sp, * (ch 1, sk 3 dc, 2 dc between last and next dc) 22 times; dc corner in corner. Rep from * around. Join, fasten off. Rnd 26: Orange, work as for rnd 13.

Rnd 27: Dark red, starting sc corner in same sp, * (ch 2, long sc between 2 pink dc below) 24 times; sc corner in corner. Rep from * around. Join, do *not* fasten off. Rnd 28: Sl st in corner sp, work as for rnd 13. Rnd 29: Pink, starting sc corner in same sp, (ch 1, sk 3 dc, 2 sc between last and next dc) 26 times; ch 1, sc corner in corner. Join, fasten off. Rnds 30 and 31: Black, work as for rnds 13 and 9. Fasten off. Fold corners to center. Sew 2 seams, stitch for stitch; slip pillow form inside; then sew rem 2 seams.

Crocheted Curtain

The airy, openwork pattern of this crocheted curtain allows sunlight to filter through while, at the same time, providing a degree of privacy for your room.

Materials

Clark's Mercerized Crochet, size 30, 250 yd. balls
  8 balls No. 135-C Tango
Size 10 steel crochet hook
1 yd. ½-inch-wide ribbon for casing

Gauge

1 repeat = 1⅝ inches, first 6 rows of main pattern = 1½ inches
Note: Basic crochet stitches are given on pages 92-93. In addition, for this project you will need to know treble crochet: Yo twice, insert hook in fifth ch of foundation ch; draw loop through. Then * yo through 2 loops; rep from * 2 more times. See drawing below.
D tr (double treble crochet): Yo three times, insert hook in sixth

ch of foundation ch; draw loop through. Then * yo through 2 loops; rep from * 3 more times.

Directions

Casing—Starting at narrow end, ch 10. Foundation row: Dc in 4th ch from hook and in each ch. Ch 2, turn. Row 1: Dc in next dc and in each dc across, dc in top of turning chain. Ch 2, turn. Rep last row until 222 rows in all have been made. At end of last row, ch 3.

Main Section—Row 1: Working over ends of rows, make 2 dc in each row across casing—445 dc, counting ch 3 as a dc. Ch 4, turn. Row 2: Tr in next 4 dc, * ch 5, sk 7 dc, in next dc make 2 d tr, 2 tr and 2 d tr, ch 5, sk 7 dc, tr in next 5 dc. Rep from * across, end with tr in last 4 dc, tr in top of turning chain. Ch 4, turn.

Row 3: Tr in next 4 tr, * ch 3, sk next sp, tr in next 3 sts, ch 7, tr in next 3 sts, ch 3, sk next sp, tr in next 5 tr. Rep from * across, end with tr in last 4 tr, tr in top of turning chain. Ch 4, turn. Row 4: Tr in next 4 tr, * ch 3, tr in next 3 tr, ch 3, 1 sc in next sp, ch 3, tr in next 3 tr, ch 3, sk next sp, tr in next 5 tr. Rep from * across, end with tr in last 4 tr, tr in top of turning chain. Ch 4, turn.

Row 5: Tr in next 4 tr, * ch 5, sk next sp, tr in next 3 tr, sk next 2 sps, tr in next 3 tr, ch 5, sk next sp, tr in next 5 tr. Rep from * across, end with tr in last 4 tr, tr in top of turning chain. Ch 4, turn. Row 6: Tr in next 4 tr, * ch 7, sk next sp, holding back on hook last loop of each st, d tr in next 2 tr, tr in next 2 tr, d tr in next 2 tr, thread over and draw through all loops on hook—cluster made; ch 7, sk next sp, tr in next 5 tr. Rep from * across, end with tr in last 4 tr, tr in top of turning chain. Ch 3, turn.

Row 7: Dc in next 4 tr, * dc in next 7 ch, dc in top of cluster, dc in next 7 ch, dc in next 5 tr. Rep from * across, end with dc in last 4 tr, dc in top of turning chain. Ch 4, turn. Rep rows 2-7 for pat until curtain measures 20 inches; end with row 7 of pat. At end of last row, ch 3, turn. Next row: Dc in next dc and in each dc across. Break off and fasten.

Pin piece to a flat surface to measurements; cover with a damp cloth and leave to dry; do not press. Sew ribbon to wrong side of casing.

Granny Square Sampler Afghan

(shown on cover, pages 4 and 5, and page 88)

This unique piece of crochet is an inspiration to granny square devotees. Make one similar to ours, based on variations of several patterns, or use just one motif throughout.

These instructions are meant to be used chiefly as guidelines to get you started on your own original sampler. You'll find ample opportunity here to give free reign to your creative talents.

Materials
Knitting worsted, 4 ply acrylic, 4 oz. skeins
  2 navy blue
  An assortment of the same type of yarn in different colors
Size H crochet hook

Finished size
46x55 inches (approximate size)
Note: If when assembling, motifs do not fit as desired, simply add on another row of crochet where needed. Some border colors are charted. Work from diagram on page 89 and use bright colors throughout.

Directions
Granny square motif (A)—Make 6.
  A-1 (1 granny square with 7 rnds): With first color ch 4; join with sl st to form ring.
  Rnd 1: Ch 3 (counts as 1 dc), 2 dc in center of ring, * ch 3, 3 dc in center of ring, rep from * 2 more times, end with ch 3; join with sl st to top of beg ch 3. End off.
  Rnd 2: With second color, in ch 3 sp of previous rnd work (ch 3, 2 dc, ch 3, 3 dc) (corner), * in next ch 3 sp work (3 dc, ch 3, 3

dc), rep from * twice, join with sl st to top of ch 3. End off.
  Rnd 3: With third color, (ch 3, 2 dc, ch 3, 3 dc) in ch 3 at corner sp, then work 3 dc between each 3 dc group on sides and (3 dc, ch 3, 3 dc) in each corner; join with sl st. End off.
  Rnds 4, 5, 6, 7: Using a different color for each row, rep instructions for rnd 3.
  A-2 (4 granny squares with 3 rnds each): Follow instructions for the first three rnds above. Whipstitch the four squares together to form one square.
  Border—With navy work 3 dc between each group of dc along edges, and (3 dc, ch 3, 3 dc) in each corner; join with sl st. End off.
  A-3 (2 granny squares with 3 rnds each): Follow instructions for the first three rnds above. Whipstitch the two squares together to form a rectangle. With brown, work border as in pattern A-2. Along one long border edge only, work 1 dc in each st. End off.
  A-4 (1 granny square with 7 rnds): Follow instructions for A-1 granny square. *Note:* Use navy for seventh rnd.
  A-5 (2 granny squares with 4 rnds each): Follow instructions for the first four rnds above. *Note:* On last rnd of one square use navy. Whipstitch squares tog to form rectangle.
  A-6 (2 granny squares with 5 rnds each): Follow instructions for the first five rnds above. *Note:* On last rnd of one square use navy. Whipstitch squares tog to form rectangle.
Star motif (B)—Make 5.
  B-1 (1 star motif with 9 rnds): Work each motif in different colors.
  Basic star square: Ch 3, sl st to 1st ch to form ring, ch 1.
  Rnd 1: * 1 sc in center of ring, ch 4, 1 sc in 2nd ch from hook, 1 sc in each of next 2 ch sts, rep

from * 4 more times (5 spoke center); join with sl st to beg sc. End off.
  Rnd 2: Attach new color in center top st of any spoke, ch 1 sc in same sp, * sk next 3 sc, (1 trc, 1 dc, 1 trc) in next sc, sl st to top of next spoke, rep from * around; join with sl st to beg sc. *Do not end off.*
  Rnd 3: * sk next st, (1 hdc, 1 dc, 1 trc, ch 1, 1 trc, 1 dc, 1 hdc) in top of next st, sk next st, sl st in top of next st, rep from * around; join with sl st to beg st. End off.
  Rnd 4: Attach another color in ch 1 back loop st at any point, * sk next 3 sts, (1 trc, 3 dc, 1 trc) in next st, sk next 3 sts, sl st in back loop of ch 1 point, rep from * around; join with sl st to beg st. End off.
  Rnd 5: Attach second color in any st, (work through both loops), 2 sc in each st around (60 sc); join with sl st to beg sc. End off.
  Rnd 6: *Note:* Work on right side in top back loops only. With star point at top, count clockwise 8 sc from point (this will be in sc above 3rd dc in rnd 4). Attach same color as rnd 2, work ch 6, 1 trc in next sc, * 1 dc in next sc, 1 hdc in each of next 2 sc, 1 sc in each of next 7 sc, 1 hdc in each of next 2 sc, 1 dc in next sc, 1 trc in next sc, ch 2, 1 trc in next sc, rep from * around; join with sl st to top of 4th ch of beg ch 6. End off.
  Rnd 7: Attach same color as rnd 4 in ch 2 corner sp, ch 3, 1 sc in same sp, * 1 sc each in next 15 sts, 1 sc in next ch 2 sp, rep from * around; join with sl st to beg sc. End off.
  Rnd 8: Attach same color used in rnd 4 in ch 2 corner, rep rnd 7 (17 sc on each side).
  Rnd 9: Attach same color as rnd 5 in any corner sp, (ch 2, 1 hdc, ch 3, 2 hdc) in same sp, * sk next sc, 2 hdc in next sc, rep from * across to next corner, * work

(2 hdc, ch 3, 2 hdc) in same corner sp, rep from * around; join with sl st to top of beg ch 2. End off.

Rnd 10: With new color work 2 hdc between groups of hdc along all edges, and (2 hdc, ch 3, 2 hdc) in each corner. End off.

B-2 (1 star motif with 4 rnds): Follow instructions for first 4 rnds above.

Rnd 5: Attach fifth color in top of 3rd dc of previous rnd, (ch 4, 2 trc, ch 3, 3 trc), in same sp, * 2 dc in next st, 1 hdc in next st, 2 sc in next st, 1 hdc in next st, 2 dc in next st*, ** (3 trc, ch 3, 3 trc), in next st, rep from * through **, 2 more times, and from * to *, 1 more time; join with sl st to beg trc. End off.

Rnd 6: Attach sixth color and work 1 sc in each st along edges, and (2 sc, ch 3, 2 sc), in each corner. End off.

Rnd 7: With navy, work * (3 dc, ch 3, 3 dc), in each corner, and sk next 2 sc, 3 dc in next sc, sk next 2 sc along edges; join with sl st to beg dc. End off.

B-3 (1 star motif with 9 rnds): Follow same directions as for pattern B-1, using a different color combination and working last rnd with navy.

B-4 (1 star motif with 9 rnds): Follow same directions as for pattern B-3.

B-5 (1 star motif with 4 rnds): Follow directions for pattern B-2, with the exception of using a different color for rnd 7.

Diamond square motif (C)— Make 5.

Note: Work all rnds in different colors.

C-1 (1 diamond square motif): Starting at center with first color, ch 4, sl st to first ch to form ring, ch 1.

Rnd 1: Work 6 sc in center of ring, join with sl st to beg sc. Do not end off.

Rnd 2: Ch 2 (counts as 1 hdc), 1 hdc in same sp, 2 hdc in top of

each sc around (12 hdc); join with sl st to beg ch 2. End off.

Rnd 3: Attach second color, ch 1, 1 sc in top of next st. * ch 1, sc in next st, rep from * around; join with sl st to beg st. End off.

Rnd 4: Attach third color in any ch 1 sp, ch 3 (counts as 1 dc), 2 dc in same sp, * 3 dc in next ch 1 sp, rep from * around (12 groups of 3 dc); join with sl st to beg dc. End off.

Rnd 5: Attach fourth color in any dc. Ch 3 (counts as 1 dc), 2 dc in same dc, ch 2, 3 dc in next dc (corner), * 1 hdc in next dc, 1 sc in each in next 5 dc, 1 hdc in next dc *, ** (3 dc in next dc, ch 2, 3 dc in next dc), rep from * through ** two more times and from * to * one more time; join with sl st to beg dc. End off.

Rnd 6: Attach fifth color in ch 2 corner sp. Work 2 sc in same sp, * 2 sc in next dc, 1 sc each in next 11 sts, 2 sc in next dc, 2 sc in corner sp, rep from * 3 more times; join with sl st to beg sc. End off.

Corners—Attach yarn to second sc before 2 sc corner, work 1 sc in same sp, and in each of next 12 sts, ch 1, turn, * decrease 1 sc, 1 sc in each st across, (decreasing 1 sc on last st), ch 1, turn, rep from * 6 more times. End off. Work three other colored corners the same way.

Border—With navy work 1 dc in each st along all of the edges, and (2 dc, ch 2, 2 dc), in each corner; join with sl st to beg dc. End off.

C-2 (1 diamond square motif): Work the same as for pattern C-1, except for different colors.

C-3 (1 diamond square motif): Work the same as for pattern C-1, except for different colors.

C-4 (1 diamond square motif): With first color ch 5, sl st to first ch to form ring.

Rnd 1: Ch 3 (counts as 1 dc), 1 dc, ch 1, 2 dc, in center of ring, * ch 3, (2 dc, ch 1, 2 dc), in center

of ring, rep from * 2 more times; ch 3, join with sl st to beg dc. End off.

Rnd 2: Attach second color to ch 3 corner sp, (ch 3, 2 dc, ch 3, 3 dc) in same sp, * ch 4, 1 long sc in center of ring, covering ch 1 sp of previous rnd, ch 4 *, ** (3 dc, ch 3, 3 dc), in next ch 3 sp, rep from * through **, 2 more times, and from * to * 1 more time, join with sl st to beg dc. End off.

Rnd 3: Attach third color to ch 3 corner sp. Work (2 sc, ch 2, 2 sc), in same sp, * 1 sc each in next 3 dc, ch 1, 1 trc in sc st in previous rnd, ch 1, 1 sc each in next 3 dc *, ** (2 sc, ch 2, 2 sc), (corner), rep from * through ** 2 more times, and from * to * 1 more time, sl st in first sc. End off.

Rnd 4: Rep directions as given for rnd 6 in C-1 substituting sc for dc, and having 9 sc instead of 11.

Corners—Rep directions as given for corners in C-1.

C-5 (1 diamond square motif): Rnds 1, 2, 3, 4: Rep directions as given for C-1.

Rnds 5, 6, 7: Work each rnd in a different color with 1 sc in each sc along all edges, and (2 sc, ch 2, 2 sc), in each corner.

Rnd 8: With navy work * (3 dc, ch 2, 2 dc), in each corner, and along each edge work sk 1 sc, 3 dc in next sc, sk 1 sc, rep from * around. End off.

Simple square motif (D)— Make 5.

D-1 (1 simple square motif): With first color, ch 11.

Row 1: 1 sc in second ch from hook, and in each ch st across (10 sc), ch 1, turn.

Row 2: 1 sc in each sc across, ch 1, turn.

Rows 3 through 15: Work as for row 2, omit ch 1 on end of row 15. End off.

Border—Rnd 1: With second color ch 3, work 1 dc in each st

continued

Granny Square Sampler Afghan *(continued)*

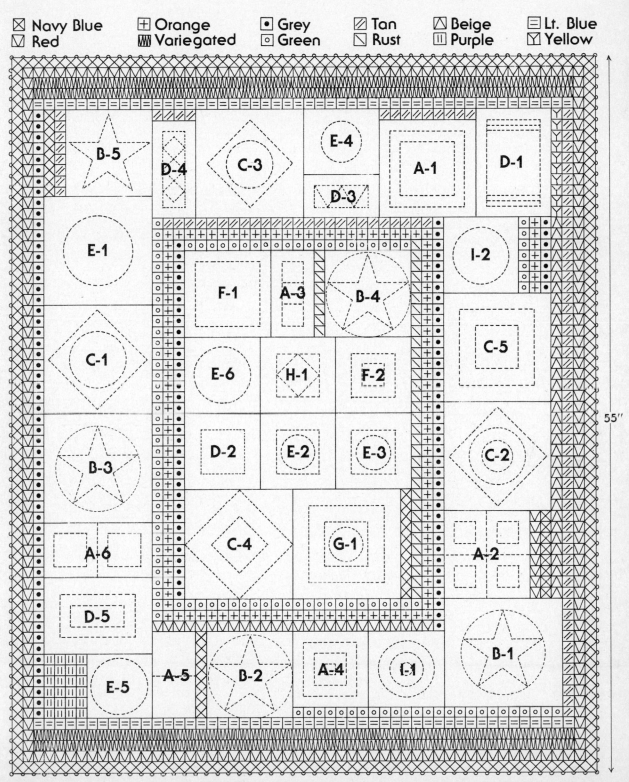

Navy Blue ⊠ Orange ⊞ Grey ⊡ Tan ▨ Beige ◁ Lt. Blue ⊟
Red ▽ Variegated ▩ Green ⊙ Rust ◩ Purple ⦀ Yellow ⊻

55″

46″

continued

Granny Square Sampler Afghan *(continued)*

around edges, and (2 dc, ch 2, 2 dc) in each corner.

Rnds 2 and 3: On each 10 sc edge, work 2 rows of 1 dc in each dc. Make each row a different color.

Rnd 4: Attach navy in corner, and work (3 dc, ch 2, 3 dc), in each corner, and 3 dc in every third st along all edges. End off.

D-2 (1 simple square motif): With first color, ch 16.

Row 1: 1 sc in second ch from hook and in each ch st across (15 sc), ch 1, turn.

Row 2: 1 sc in each sc across (15 sc), ch 1, turn.

Rows 3 through 15: Rep row 2. End off.

Border—Rnd 1: With second color work 1 sc in each st along edges, and (2 sc, ch 2, 2 sc) in each corner. End off.

Rnd 2: Rep rnd 1 with a new color.

Rnd 3: Work (3 dc, ch 2, 3 dc), in each corner, and 3 dc in every third st along all edges. End off.

D-3 (1 simple square motif): With first color, ch 16.

Row 1: With first color make sc in ea of the first 2 sts, * change color, sc in ea of next 2 sts, change to first color, make 2 sc in ea of next 2 sts, rep from * across chain.

Row 2: Sc in ea sc across, having second color over first color. Repeat rows 1 and 2 for total of 5 rows.

Borders—Rep rnds 1, 2, 3 as given in D-2 border directions.

D-4 (1 simple square motif): Rows 1 through 20: Rep directions as given for D-1, but extend rows to the count of 20.

Border—Rep rnds 1, 2, 3 as given in D-2 for borders.

Design—With another color, work embroidery in cross-stitch in diamond shape across center of sc panel.

D-5 (1 simple square motif): Rep directions given for D-4 for 20 rnds and including 1, 2, 3 border rnds.

Rnd 4: Work (3 dc, ch 2, 3 dc) in each corner, and 3 dc between each dc group along edges. End off.

Design—Work embroidery in cross-stitch in zigzag pattern across center of sc panel.

Circle motif (E)—Make 6.

E-1 (1 circle motif): With first color ch 4, sl st in 1st ch to form ring.

Rnd 1: Ch 1, work 12 sc in center of ring; join with sl st to beg sc, do not end off.

Rnd 2: *Note:* Work in both loops. Ch 3 (counts as 1 dc), 2 dc in same sp, ch 1 * sk next sc, 3 dc in next sc, ch 1, rep from * around (6 groups of 3 dc); join with sl st to beg dc. Do not end off.

Rnd 3: Work 1 sl st in top of next dc, ch 3, 1 dc in same sp, * ch 1, sk next dc, 2 dc in next ch 1 sp, ch 1, sk next dc, 2 dc in next dc, rep from * around (12 groups of 2 dc), ch 1, join with sl st to beg dc. End off.

Rnd 4: Attach second color in ch 1 sp. Ch 3 (counts as first dc). Work * (3 dc, ch 3, 3 dc), in same sp (corner), 3 dc bet next group of 2 dc, 2 times, rep from * 3 more times; join with sl st to beg dc. End off.

Rnd 5: Attach third color. Work 1 sc in each st and between groups of dc, and in each corner work 1 sc, ch 3, 1 sc; join with sl st to beg sc. End off.

Rnd 6: Attach navy in ch 3 corner. Ch 3 (counts as first dc). Work * (2 dc in same sp, ch 3, 3 dc), in corner sp *, ** sk next 2 sts, 3 dc in next st, rep from along edge to next corner, rep from * through ** around; join with sl st to beg dc. End off.

E-2 (1 circle motif): Work in solid color as in directions for E-1 for 5 rnds. Work sixth rnd in navy.

E-3 (1 circle motif): Work 5 rnds as in directions for E-1,

except work each rnd in a different color.

6th rnd: Work in navy.

E-4 (1 circle motif): Work in solid color for 3 rnds only as given in directions for E-1.

Rnd 4: Attach second color in ch 1 sp. Ch 3 (counts as first dc), make * (3 dc, ch 2, 3 dc), in same sp (corner), work ** 3 dc bet next group of dc in previous rnd, 2 times, rep from * through ** 3 more times. End off.

Rnd 5: With navy work 1 dc in each st along each edge, and (2 dc, ch 2, 2 dc) in each corner. End off.

E-5 (1 circle motif): Work same motif as in directions E-3.

E-6 (1 circle motif): Work same motif as in directions E-3.

Variation motif (F)—Make 2.

F-1 (1 variation motif): With first color ch 4, sl st in 1st ch to form ring.

Rnd 1: Ch 3 (counts as 1 dc), 4 dc in center of ring, * ch 5, 4 dc in ring, rep from * 2 more times, ch 5; join with sl st to beg dc. End off.

Rnd 2: Attach second color in ch 5 sp. Work * (3 dc, ch 3, 3 dc) (corner sp), ch 1, sk next 2 dc, (1 dc, ch 1, 1 dc), between second and third dc, rep from * 3 more times; join with sl st to beg dc. End off.

Rnd 3: Attach third color in ch 3 corner sp. Work * (3 dc, ch 3, 3 dc) in same sp, ch 2, 1 dc in ch 1 sp, ch 1, 3 dc in next sc sp, ch 1, 1 dc in next ch 1 sp, ch 2, rep from * 3 more times; join with sl st to beg dc. End off.

Rnd 4: Attach fourth color in ch 2 corner sp. Work * (3 dc, ch 3, 3 dc), in same sp, 3 dc in next ch 2 sp, ch 2, 2 dc in top of center dc of 3 dc group of previous rnd, ch 1, 3 dc in next ch 2 sp, rep from * 3 more times; join with sl st to beg dc. End off.

Rnd 5: Attach fifth color to ch 3 corner sp, work * (3 dc, ch 3, 3 dc) in same corner sp, sk next

2 dc, 3 dc in top of next dc, sk next dc, 3 dc in top of next dc, sk next dc, 3 dc in top of next dc, sk next dc, 3 dc in top of next dc, sk next 2 dc, rep from * 3 more times. End off.

F-2 (1 variation motif): Rep directions as for F-1.

Big Square Motif (G)—Make 1.

Starting at center with first color ch 4, sl st to first ch to form ring, ch 1.

Rnd 1: Work 6 sc in center of ring, join with sl st to beg sc. Do not end off.

Rnd 2: Ch 2 (counts as 1 hdc), 1 hdc in same sp, 2 hdc in top of each sc around (12 hdc); join with sl st to beg ch 2. End off.

Rnd 3: Attach second color, ch 1, 1 sc in top of next st, * ch 1, sc in next st, rep from * around; join with sl st to beg sc. End off.

Rnd 4: Attach third color in any ch 1 sp, ch 3 (counts as 1 dc), 2 dc in same sp, * 3 dc in next ch 1 sp, rep from * around (12 groups of 3 dc); join with sl st to beg dc. End off.

Rnd 5: Attach fourth color between any dc group, * ch 3, 1 sc between next group of dc, rep from * around; join with sl st to beg st. End off.

Rnd 6: Attach fifth color in any ch 3 sp, (ch 3, 2 dc, ch 3, 3 dc), in same sp (corner), * 3 dc in next 2 ch 3 sps, (3 dc, ch 3, 3 dc), in next ch 3 sp, rep from * around. End off.

Rnd 7: Attach sixth color in ch 3 corner. Work (3 dc, ch 3, 3 dc) in each ch 3 corner and 3 dc between each dc group along all edges. End off.

Rnds 8 and 9: Attach seventh color, work 1 dc in top of each st along edges and (1 dc, ch 3, 1 dc), in each corner. End off.

Rnd 10: Attach eighth color and rep directions as for rnd 7.

Violet Motif (H)—Make 1.

Start at center with yellow, ch 4, sl st to beg ch to form ring.

Rnd 1: * 1 sc in center of ring, ch 4, rep from * 3 more times; join with sl st to beg sc. End off.

Rnd 2: Attach lavender in sc st, 1 sl st in same sp, * (1 sc, 1 hdc, 1 dc, 1 hdc, 1 sc), in next ch 4 sp, 1 sl st in next sc (petal), rep from * 3 more times; join with sl st to beg sl st. End off.

Rnd 3: Attach green to back loop of sc in any petal, ch 3 (counts as 1 dc), 1 dc, ch 3, 2 dc, in same sp, 2 dc in back loop of next hdc in previous rnd, * ch 1, sk next 3 sts in previous rnd, 2 dc in back loop of next hdc, (2 dc, ch 3, 2 dc), in back loop of dc, 2 dc in back loop of next hdc, rep from * 2 more times; join with sl st to top of beg dc. End off.

Rnd 4: Attach lavender and work 1 hdc in each st along all edges and (2 hdc, ch 3, 2 hdc) in each ch 3 corner. End off.

Rnd 5: Attach white in ch 3 corner, (ch 3, 1 dc, ch 3, 2 dc), in same sp, * sk next hdc sp, 2 dc in next hdc, rep from * along all edges and (2 dc, ch 3, 2 dc), in each ch 3 corner. End off.

Rnd 6: Attach navy, work 3 dc between each dc group along all edges with (3 dc, ch 3, 3 dc), in each ch 3 corner; join with sl st to beg dc. End off.

Rose motif (I)—Make 2.

I-1 (1 rose motif): With first color ch 4, sl st to first ch to form ring.

Rnd 1: Work 8 sc in center of ring; join with sl st to beg sc.

Rnd 2: Ch 3 (counts as 1 dc), 4 dc in same sc sp, drop loop from hook, * insert hook from front to back of work in first dc of the 5 dc group, draw dropped loop through, ch 1 to fasten, (petal made), ch 3, 5 dc in next sc, rep from * 6 more times (8 petals), ch 3; join with sl st to beg dc. End off.

Rnd 3: Attach second color in ch 3 sp, (ch 3, 2 dc), in same sp, * dc in next ch 1 sp, 3 dc in next ch 3 sp, rep from * around (32 dc); join with sl st to beg dc. End off.

Rnd 4: Note: Work in top back loop only. Attach third color in dc back loop, (ch 3, 1 dc, ch 1, 2 dc), in same sp, * 1 dc in next dc, 1 hdc in each of next 2 dc, 1 sc in next dc, 1 hdc in each of next 2 dc, 1 dc in next dc, ** (2 dc, ch 1, 2 dc) in next dc, rep from * through ** 2 more times, and from * to * one more time; join with sl st to beg dc. End off.

Rnd 5: Attach fourth color, work 1 sc in each st along edges, and (1 sc, ch 2, 1 sc), in each corner ch 1 sp; join with sl st to beg sc. End off.

Rnd 6: Attach navy in ch 2 corner, (ch 3, 2 dc, ch 3, 3 dc), in same sp, * sk next sc, 3 dc in next sc *, rep from * to next corner, ** (3 dc, ch 3, 3 dc), in same sp, rep from * through ** 2 more times, and from * to * 1 more time; join with sl st to beg dc. End off.

I-2 (1 rose motif): Work motif same as I-1, but work rnd 6 with bright color. Add 3 rows of dc in bright colors to one side of motif to finish.

Afghan assembly—Following diagram on pages 88-89, whipstitch center motifs together first. Note: If squares do not fit as desired, simply add another row of dc.

Borders—Rnds 1, 2, 3: Make each border rnd a different color. Work 3 dc in every third st along all edges, and (3 dc, ch 3, 3 dc) in each corner.

Whipstitch the rest of squares according to diagram in same manner. Add as many borders as desired to edge afghan, by working in same manner as described for borders around center motif squares.

On last border of afghan, work a picot st between each 3 dc group to finish. Work 1 sc, * ch 3, sl st in top of sc just made (picot st), sc in next 3 sts, picot, rep from * around border.

Basic Crochet Stitches

Crochet Abbreviations

beg	begin(ning)
bet	between
ch	chain
dc	double crochet
dec	decrease
dtr	double treble
hdc	half double crochet
inc	increase
lp(s)	loop(s)
pat	pattern
rnd	round
sc	single crochet
sl st	slip stitch
sp	space
st(s)	stitch(es)
tog	together
yo	yarn over

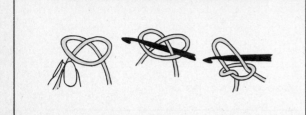

Start by making a slip knot on crochet hook about 6 inches from end of yarn. Pull one end of yarn to tighten knot.

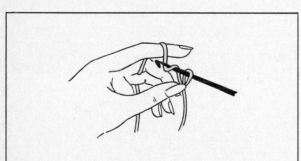

Hold the hook between right index finger and thumb, as you would a pencil. Wrap yarn over ring finger, under middle finger and over index finger, holding short end between thumb and index finger. If you need more tension, wrap yarn around little finger. Insert hook under and over strand of yarn.

Make the foundation chain by catching strand with hook and drawing it through loop. Make the chain as long as pattern calls for.

Single crochet: Insert the hook into the second chain from the hook, under two upper strands of yarn.

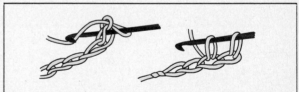

Draw up a loop.

Draw yarn over hook.

Pull yarn through the two loops, completing single crochet stitch. Insert hook into next stitch, and repeat last four steps.

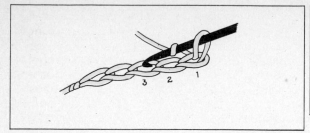

Half double crochet: With yarn over hook, insert hook into third chain, under the two upper strands of yarn.

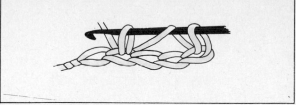

Draw up a loop.

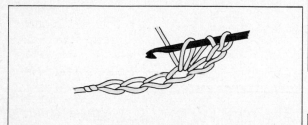

Draw up a loop.

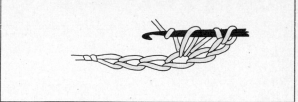

Wrap yarn over hook.

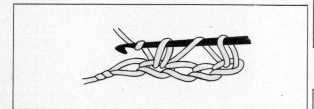

Draw yarn over the hook.

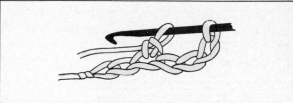

Draw yarn through two loops.

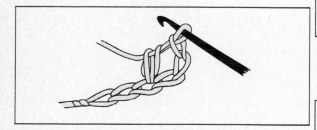

Pull through the 3 loops, completing the half double crochet.

Yarn over again and through last two loops on hook. This completes double crochet.

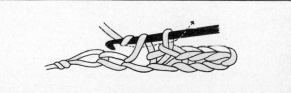

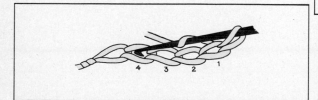

Double crochet: Holding yarn over hook, insert hook into fourth chain, under the two upper strands of yarn.

Slip stitch: After you've made the foundation chain, insert the crochet hook under the top strand of the second chain from the hook, and yarn over. With a single motion, pull the yarn through the stitch and loop on the hook. Insert the hook under the top strand of the next chain, then yarn over and draw the yarn through stitch and loop on hook. Repeat this procedure to the end of the chain.

Basic Knitting Stitches

Knitting Abbreviations

k	knit
p	purl
st(s)	stitch(es)
tog	together
pat	pattern
inc	increase
dec	decrease
beg	beginning
sp	space
rnd	round
yo	yarn over
rem	remaining
rep	repeat
sk	skip
st st	stockinette stitch
MC	main color
CC	contrasting color
sl st	slip stitch
psso	pass slip st over
dp	double-pointed

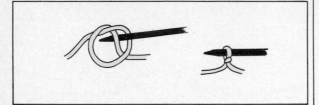

To cast on, make a slip knot around needle at a distance from yarn end that equals one inch for each stitch to be cast on.

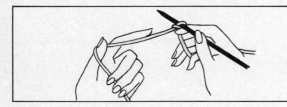

Hold needle that has slip knot in your right hand and make a loop of the short length of yarn around your left thumb.

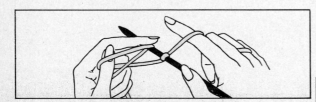

Insert point of needle in your right hand under loop on your left thumb. Loop yarn from ball over fingers of your right hand.

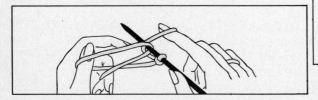

Wind yarn from ball under and over needle and draw it through loop, leaving the stitch on the needle.

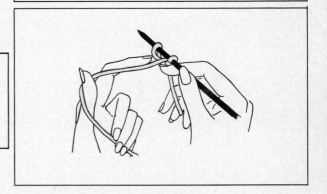

Tighten stitches on needle and bring yarn end around thumb so it is ready for next stitch. Repeat the last four steps until you have desired number of stitches. Switch needle with cast-on stitches to left hand.

To make a knit stitch, hold needle with stitches in left hand and other needle in right hand. Insert right needle through stitch on left needle from front to back. Pass yarn around point of right needle to form loop.

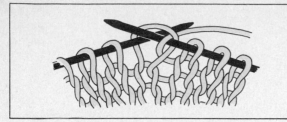

Pull this loop through stitch on left needle, and draw loop onto right needle.

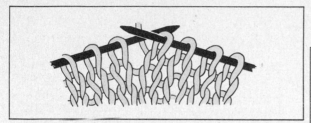

Now, slip the stitch completely off of the left needle. Repeat these steps until you have transferred all of the stitches from the left needle to the right needle. This completes one row of knitting. When you start working on the next row, move needle holding stitches to your left hand, and free the needle to your right hand.

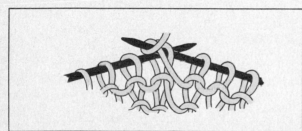

To make a purl stitch, hold the needle with the stitches in your left hand and the other needle in your right hand. Insert the right needle through the stitch on the left needle from back to front. Wind the yarn around the point of the right needle to form a loop.

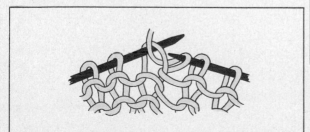

Draw a loop through the stitch on the needle in your left hand, and transfer it to the needle in your right hand.

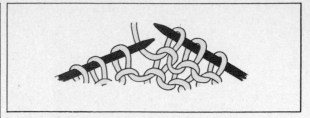

Slip stitch completely off left needle. Repeat these steps until all loops on left needle have been transferred to right needle. This completes one row of purling. Switch needles and work next row.

In order to increase a stitch, knit or purl as usual, but do not slip it off the left needle. Instead, insert right needle into back of stitch and knit or purl into stitch a second time. Slip both onto right needle, resulting in two stitches. To decrease, knit or purl two stitches together at the same time. To slip a stitch, insert the right needle as If to purl (unless directions read to do it as if to knit). Then slip stitch onto right needle without working; be careful not to twist stitch.

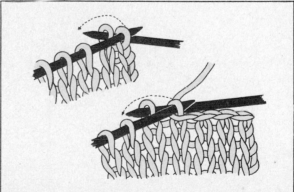

To bind off, work two stitches in pattern loosely. With left needle, lift first stitch over second stitch and off right needle. This binds off one stitch. Repeat this same technique for required number of stitches. If you are binding off an entire row, continue until one stitch remains; break yarn and draw end through the last stitch.

Designers

We are happy to acknowledge our indebtedness and express our sincere thanks to the following people for their valuable help in producing this book.

Jackie H. Curry _____ 4-5, 6-7, 48-49, 86-87
Mary Jo Sandell _____ 8-9
Susan Toplitz _____ 15, 36-37
Winnie Juhl _____ 20-21
Mary Walker Phillips _____ 22-23, 32-33, 66-67
May Griffin _____ 28-29
Connie Lidster _____ 30-31
Marie Muth _____ 34-35
Marie B. Schulz _____ 50-51
Christine Kaczmarczyk _____ 54-55, 78-79
Judy Solomon _____ 62-63, 74-75
Gary Boling _____ 66-67
Judy Lueke _____ 78-79

Acknowledgments

Emile Bernat & Sons Co. ____ 10-11, 12-13-14, 44-45
William Unger & Co., Inc. _____ 16-17
Bernard Ulmann _____ 18-19
Frederick J. Fawcett Co. _____ 32
Coats & Clark _____ 85
Betty Crist
Pat Doviddio
Grace Towner

A number of family treasures were loaned to us that we might share them with you. They appeared through the courtesy of the following people:

Mary Jane Linderman _____ 24-25-26
Mona Mortensen _____ 27, 40-41
Some Place, Inc.
    Berkeley, California _____ 68-69, 72-73, 33